YOU AND YOUR AURA

Brings science and metaphysics together to
present an easy to understand overview of
the human aura.

YOU AND YOUR AURA

Joseph Ostrom

Illustrated by the author

THE AQUARIAN PRESS
Wellingborough, Northamptonshire

First published 1987

British Library Cataloguing in Publication Data

Ostrom, Joseph
You and your aura.
1. Aura
I. Title
133.9'2   BF1389.A8

ISBN 0-85030-549-7

*The Aquarian Press is part of the
Thorsons Publishing Group*

Printed and bound in Great Britain by
Hazell Watson & Viney Limited,
Member of the BPCC Group,
Aylesbury, Bucks

Contents

Dedication

This book is dedicated to my wife Carol without whose devotion, encouragement and tireless editing, it would not have been possible; and to my daughter, Isadora, who gave up her daddy for several precious months.

Thanks to Gary Raham, a delightful sceptic, for his insights into things scientific.

Disclaimer

The material in this book is presented for educational and informational purposes only. It is not intended to replace established medical diagnostic procedures or treatment. The author and publishers are in no way responsible for those individuals who choose not to heed this disclaimer.

Foreword

A large oak, its leaves rattling in the warm summer breeze, lays its cool shadow on a young boy. His feet dangle lazily over the sandy bank at the edge of a small pond. The boy's eyes watch colourful rainbows dance off the top of a nearby rock. A squirrel, surrounded in a cocoon of blue and green light, peels away at an acorn near the rock. The boy extends his hand offering more acorns and the squirrel darts quickly to the far side of the old oak. Jets of light pour out of the boy's fingertips. Over two decades would pass before he would discover that not everybody saw things as he did.

That boy was me. He was some of you as well.

In my lectures I usually start out by asking for a show of hands from those in the audience who see, or think they have seen, an aura. Now granted, a lecture on the aura will draw a very specific audience, but these people come from all walks of life, all disciplines, almost every stratum of society. When I began asking this question a few years back, the response was that approximately one third of the audience had seen what they thought was an aura at least once in their life. Now I find that the percentage has risen to almost half.

Most of those who had had the experience said they had only seen an aura once or twice, often during a church service or in the hospital after surgery. Others have reported seeing coloured light 'growing' off performers at a concert.

While it is possible that someone coming out of anaesthesia may be having drug-induced perceptions, and in the case of the concert performer, lighting mastery can create the effect, many others have reported rather ordinary and unexpected auric sightings around a spouse or a friend. Mothers of newborns report seeing a beautiful green or blue glow around their babies.

The large concert hall was filled with flower children bedecked in cossack shirts, beads, flowers and long hair. As Ravi Shankar, Kamala and Alla Rakha played through a portion of their first raga, they could smell the pungent odours of burning marijuana floating up to them on the stage. Ravi cut the raga short and announced to the audience that he would not continue the performance as long as people were getting high. He said that the expression of his music was sacred and that one did not need drugs to experience the spiritual upliftment contained within its expression. The smoking stopped and the concert continued.

In a few moments I began to understand what he had meant. The colours around Shankar and the others in the group began to merge. I had seen the colours around people merge before, but this was different. As the colours blended with one another, they began to create just one colour — a bright violet.

My first thought was that it was a very clever creation by the lighting director, perhaps an expanding field on each of the performer's key-lights through a violet gel, or maybe a follow-spot subtly rising in brightness. As the concert continued the bright violet glow grew in intensity and size, engulfing the performers as if they were sitting in a large bonfire.

I blinked my eyes a few times and the violet flames were gone. I glanced up at the banks of lights just above the stage; to my surprise they were white lights. In fact the lighting scheme was very simple, even the follow-spot was white.

I shifted my attention back to the performance. Again the violet light formed around Ravi Shankar and his group, growing until it filled the entire stage and poured out into the audience. It was beautiful, a religious experience as promised.

I was still twelve years away from knowing that what I was perceiving were the effects of the human auric field.

Eleven years later I met a woman at a party who gave me a tarot reading. She predicted that I was about to meet a woman and fall in love. The relationship was to be very important for my growth, my life would be forever changed. The tarot reader and I began to date and soon we were living together.

My interest in the metaphysical to that time had been only slight. I had studied Buddhism and had a superficial interest in astrology. For the most part my interests were physical: a loaf of bread, a jug of wine and . . . Now that Connie was in my life all of that began to change. She seemed to be a catalyst for me, psychic events began occurring. Then all too soon Connie decided to end our relationship. She moved out. I was devastated.

For several weeks I tried to convince her to come back but to no avail. I was becoming a nuisance, no longer welcome at her new apartment. The only neutral ground where we could be together was at the home of a mutual friend on Sunday afternoons at an informal gathering of people interested in metaphysical subjects.

One Sunday the topic of discussion was the human aura. After listening to everyone talk about it for a short time I realized that they must be talking about the colours that I saw around things. I thought that it was odd that they had not always seen colours around things.

'I see colours around things,' I stated and a new era began for me with those words.

'Tell us what you see. What do you see around me?' asked one woman.

I began describing what I was seeing around her. I could see by the expression on her face that she didn't really understand what I was describing. My father had spent a lot of money on my art school education. I decided that it was time to use it. I made a quick sketch of the woman and drew in various areas of light that I saw coming off her. Next to these shapes I made notations like — light blue here, green here — and drew little arrows to the corresponding areas. When I was finished I handed the drawing to the woman.

Everyone gathered around her with great curiosity. I could see that they liked the picture. Then the woman looked up from the sketch and said, 'What does it mean?'

'How should I know?'

'But you do know,' another woman added, 'you have carried this information with you from past lives.'

Past lives? What was she talking about? We hadn't covered that subject yet. I insisted that I had no idea what the picture meant. The woman (whose psychic abilities I greatly respected) continued saying that I could interpret the little sketch.

After several minutes of resistance I gave in. 'All right, I'll interpret the drawing. Not because I can, but just to get you off my back!'

I stumbled clumsily through the interpretation saying whatever came into my head. I knew that I couldn't possibly be making any sense. I hoped that my off-the-cuff interpretation would be so ridiculous that everyone would see that I was right, that I couldn't interpret what I was seeing around people.

When I had finished my ramblings there was a silence in the room. The woman whose picture I had just 'interpreted' sat staring at me in wonder.

'It's very accurate,' she said finally, 'you came up with things about me that nobody knows about.'

Over the next weeks I continued to attend the metaphysical discussion group and each week someone would ask me to draw his or her aura. One Sunday I was given a box of coloured pencils and a couple of sketch pads by one of the women. Colour, a new dimension in my aura portrait work, took this project a step further. My sketches became more detailed. My interpretations continued to surprise me. How could I possibly be able to know the things about these people that I did seem to know? Was there some truth to this past life stuff?

One Sunday I was informed that there was going to be a psychic fair in town. The other members of the discussion group thought that I should sign up. It would be a great opportunity for me to see how I would fare with complete strangers.

'Me? Do my aura portraits in public?' The idea was preposterous. I could just see myself sitting there at the fair with twelve little old gypsy ladies, black cats all over the place. I didn't want the community in which I had to go on living thinking that I was some sort of freak. 'No, thank you,' I declared, 'I don't want to join the circus!'

I was wrong about what psychic fairs are like. I have found over the years that 'psychics' come in all shapes and sizes and from all walks of life. Most of them I have met have been housewives, businessmen, production-line workers, psychologists, nurses, ministers — you name it, and use their psychic talents whenever they get the chance because they care about people and want to help to make a difference in the world.

As you may have guessed, I did sign up to work at the fair. One, it was for a charity — 40 per cent of my earnings at the fair were to go to the Cerebral Palsy Foundation. Two, maybe I could actually help people with their problems — hadn't I been helpful in the discussion group? Three, I was curious.

In the week preceding the fair, I read every book I could get my hands on that dealt with auras and colour interpretation. It was all right to trust my intuition in the discussion group, but out in the 'real' world I needed facts.

Hard facts surrounding the subject of the aura are hard to come by and so are books. Most of the really important books on the subject were written around the end of the nineteenth century and beginning of the twentieth. The early experimenters such as Dr Kilner, Oscar Bagnall, C.W. Leadbeater and others wrote about a very simple-looking auric field. To my eyes the auric field is quite complex. Was it possible that I was seeing more of this field than had ever been reported before? Or was I simply getting ready for a padded room?

I slept very little the night before the fair. My confidence was slipping with each new paragraph of new information about auric fields. By morning I was unable to remember a thing that I had learned. At ten o'clock I was spreading out my pencils and paper in an out-of-the-way dark corner of the fair, hoping that no one would see my poor, tired, shaky figure there.

I sat for an hour or so with no customers, then someone found me — a pale thin woman in her early seventies with a sadness in her eyes. When she sat down across from me she began to cry.

'I think I'm dying,' she sobbed. 'I'm afraid to die!'

Her helpless, pleading eyes burned deeply into my soul. My heart crawled into my throat. What could I possibly do or say to help this woman? My colourful little pictures seemed quite insignificant now. There were no words in my mouth for this woman. I turned pale. I wanted to run. Then a phrase that Connie had often used fell into my mind: LET GO, AND LET GOD.

I relaxed and began to examine the woman's aura. It was dim and the bands were narrow. I saw nothing in the aura that looked like disease. The woman seemed simply to lack vitality and was run down. I asked her about her physical activity and diet. Was she working or doing any kind of regular volunteer work? Did she have an interesting hobby? Had she given up on life? She had. I told her that her aura looked perfectly healthy, just a little run down. She could continue living if she chose to. I told her about a thing called colour breathing that would help to improve her vitality (I had read about it only the night before). She tried it while we talked and felt better immediately.

When the reading was over the woman had colour in her face and she was smiling. She had affirmed to live. When she left she looked a good ten years younger. I felt great! From that reading on to the present I was hooked on helping by use of my aura portraits.

1

Questions

There are several questions that almost always come up at my lectures. While the aura has been studied and perceived for many centuries, I find that the average person knows very little about the subject. The following is a collection of the most frequently asked questions and my answers to them.

Q *What is the Aura?*
A An aura is a collection of electro-magnetic energies of varying densities which are exiting from the physical, vital, etheric, mental, emotional and spiritual bodies. These particles of energy are suspended around the human body in an oval-shaped field. This oval field or 'auric egg' stands out from the body some 2-3 ft (1m) (on average) on all sides. It is also found above the head and extends below the feet into the ground.

Another 'auric egg' can be found floating above the lower 'auric egg'. It can be found anywhere from just at the edge of the lower auric bodies to 50 ft (15m) above them. This separate auric field is called the higher auric bodies.

Q *What does the aura look like to you?*
A I always see the auric bodies in cross-section much like the layers of an onion that has been sliced down the middle.

Each layer tells me something different about the person that I am viewing. The first three inner layers represent health matters and personality. The outer two layers are indicators of what is going on within the mental and emotional life of the person.

The auric bands are translucent and colourful, appearing much like the colours in a rainbow, only more subtle in intensity.

How bright these colours will seem to me varies with each individual. Some stand out like neon lights and others are so dim that it takes special viewing conditions and a great deal of concentration on my part to see them.

Several years ago I worked on a television series called 'High Chapparral'. It was a western filmed in Tucson, Arizona, where I was living at the time. I was employed as what is called a 'whistler'. I kept the audience that gathered during the shooting quiet while the cameras filmed and made sure tourists on the set stayed away from the stars.

There were a lot of actors and actresses in that production with very big personalities, each one of them had very bright and large auric fields. The filming day started early, usually around seven. As the actors came onto the set for make-up call I could see a great deal of colour emanating from them. They, however, were overshadowed by the emanations from the star of the show, Lief Erikson. When he walked onto the set his aura filled every corner with brilliant light. His presence commanded the attention of cast and crew alike. He didn't have to say a word, everyone could sense his presence as he appeared.

Occasionally I will see people like him on the street or in a restaurant. No special conditions are needed to see them, no concentration. They stick out like sore thumbs for all to see.

Over the years I have learned to control and tune out my auric sight. I don't like to eavesdrop on a person's life. I don't feel that it is morally right to analyze the factors in a person's aura unless I am asked to by that person or unless I feel that it is necessary for my own protection. Sometimes, as in the case of Lief Erikson, I can't help seeing the aura.

Q *How does the eye perceive the aura?*
A There are some 137 million receptors (7 million cones, 130 million rods) in each eye. Some of these receptors, the cones, are for focused day-vision. These cone-shaped receptors are the origin of colour vision.

There is some evidence that modern human beings see a larger variety of colours than their ancestors. Homer has described the Aegean Sea as being 'wine-dark' — a dark red? In my travel to the Greek Islands I have spent a lot of time looking at the sea; believe me, it's a very beautiful light blue-green. It is said that Aristotle saw only reds, greens and yellows. Were the Greeks colour blind? It seems unlikely. Those who are usually have difficulty seeing reds, not blues. The perception of blues seems to be a more recent development for human beings.

Perhaps if our vision is truly expanding the future may hold some visual surprises as we begin to see in the infra-red and ultra-violet ends of the spectrum. Insects are known to see patterns invisible to humans because they lie outside our visible spectrum in the ultra-violet. A time-traveller from Aristotle's era visiting an art gallery in New York in the year 2585 AD might find a room full of people admiring the bold strokes and vivid colours of what he might perceive as empty canvases.

The other type of receptor in the eye is called the rod. Rods are most prevalent in the outer regions of the receptor field. They are most sensitive as the intensity levels of lights are reduced. They are the source of our ability to see in the dark. Rods are the receptors for our peripheral vision. Under conditions of low light, the rods are coated with a substance called *visual purple* (rhodopsin). Visual purple, which is actually a magenta red, is very light sensitive and bleaches out quickly as light strikes the receptor. As low light returns to the eye, the visual purple resynthesizes itself. It is with this peripheral vision in low-light conditions that the rods perceive the aura.

Q *Can anyone see auras?*
A I believe that as small children we were all able to see auras as well as having other so-called 'psychic' gifts. It is only through conditioning by parents, teachers and society in general to conform to an established social pattern that children 'lose' these talents. How often have you heard a parent tell a child that it is not right to have imaginary friends, or that some things are real and some just a product of a childish imagination?

A few years back, a popular psychology magazine ran an article which speculated on what young children perceived of the world. It used children's drawings to gather evidence that children may be seeing things that adults do not perceive. The article showed that many children draw rainbow colours around the stick figures representing people. When the children were asked why there were colours around the people in their pictures, they were unable, through lack of language mastery, to explain what they had drawn. Adult authorities may then proceed to tell the children that there aren't really rainbows around people and soon the rainbows disappear from the children's drawings. In this way auric sight may have gone the way of many of the other subtler impressions that the brain was able to perceive before prejudiced thinking became the pattern.

I believe that I retained my ability to see auras because my teachers always encouraged me to express my creativity and artistic talents in school. Imagine what kind of a world we could create if we encouraged our children to express freely what they are perceiving.

I believe that most of us can be retrained to see auras. This belief has been reinforced time and again in my seminars. Often, in just one session, I have seen a large percentage of those in attendance begin to see some form of aura around people.

Q *Have you ever seen anyone who didn't have an aura?*
A The absence of auric light around a person represents impending death. It is my feeling that the aura is still there, but it is just too dim for me to see it.

When I was about twelve years old my grandmother became very ill. It was winter and the sidewalks were covered in ice, so my mother asked me to walk my grandmother out to the car so that she could be taken to the hospital.

Even in those days, before I knew about auras, I sensed a darkness or absence of the light around her. My grandmother had been hospitalized before and she had come back, but this time a part of me knew that she would not be returning, although my parents thought she would be home soon.

After she was driven away on that cold morning, I went behind the house and cried for a very long time. Grandmother never returned. At her funeral I was sad but I did not cry, I had already mourned the loss.

A couple of years ago my wife and I were having dinner in a Chinese restaurant. A man walked by; there was something strange about him. When he walked by our table again I purposely looked at his aura. I lost my appetite. There was no aura, only a hollow emptiness. The man was about to die. I wondered if he knew it.

After struggling with my feelings for a while, I decided to send the man a little prayer of release. I wished him a smooth transition from this world to the next and then I released him to his destiny. Soon my appetite returned and I got back to my egg rolls.

A short time later the man reappeared, this time leaving the restaurant with his party. As he walked near our table he stopped briefly and smiled warmly at me. A part of him must have known that I knew. I've always wondered what he saw when he looked at me. Did I look like the hooded Grim Reaper?

Shortly before his death, Edgar Cayce wrote a small pamphlet entitled, simply, *Auras*. In it he told a story about a time when he was shopping in a department store. He was on the sixth floor and had pushed the elevator button to go down. When the elevator arrived he saw that it was quite full. Yet there was a dark emptiness that he felt inside. Just then his attention was pulled away by a red sweater nearby. He motioned the elevator on, saying that he would catch another. Moments later the cable snapped and its occupants were plunged to their deaths. Cayce was saved by a red sweater, a colour that was not a particular favourite. of his. He realized later that what he had observed in that elevator was the absence of auric light around the ill-fated occupants. This brings up the question of predetermined events. Can we really know when we or those around us will die?

For many years I was a white-knuckle passenger on aeroplanes. All that has changed now that I understand that I perceive auras. When I get into my seat on a plane I always look around to see if all of the passengers have auras. If there is a light pouring off everyone then I buckle up my seatbelt and relax. So far I have always seen the light, and I pray I never have the experience of seeing the empty darkness. I wonder how I would react. Would I tell others aboard what I was perceiving, or would I just stand up and silently leave the plane? I hope I never find an answer to that question.

Q *Is there a difference between the auras of men and women?*
A There is not much difference between the two auras. In my consultations I see more women than men, probably because women are, at this time in history, more open to the metaphysical world. Men in general seem more controlled by the conditioning of our society and tend to shy away from exploring the psychic world. This seems to be changing as men begin to open up and understand other facets of their world.

The only difference that I have seen between the auras of men and women is that a woman's aura bulges slightly more at the hips than a man's does.

Q *What does a baby's aura look like?*
A The aura of a newborn baby is very clear and bright. Often the predominant colours are a light blue or green.

My wife Carol and I had the unforgettable experience of helping our close friends deliver their baby. My job was to photograph the process. I had three cameras hanging around my neck and was positioned just behind the midwife. After almost twenty-four hours of waiting and labour the baby finally crowned and emerged from its mother. I was surprised to note that when the baby's head came out there was no aura. It wasn't until the shoulders had emerged that the aura seemed to flash on as if a switch had been thrown. That would seem to back up my belief that the spiritual essence of the child is in and out of the foetus throughout the *in utero* period, coming into the baby to stay permanently only at the time of birth.

A baby's aura is very simple and uncluttered compared with an adult aura. There appear to be only three bands around newborns compared with the five bands in the adult's lower auric bodies.

In the first few days a baby's aura seems to trail off the top of the head like a pointed knitted ski-hat might fly out behind the head of a downhill racer. The adult aura, on the other hand, is rounded at the top of the head.

The crown chakra (see p. 52) is located at the top or crown of the head. It is the portal through which the Universal energy enters the human system. This portal also handles the outflow of energy back to the Source. It is the nearest connection to Higher Worlds that our physical body has.

In the case of a newborn's aura flowing off and fading into the distance, it seems to me that there is still a connection to the reality from which this little Soul has come. It may be that this newly-arrived Spirit needs a support system for a while as it makes its transition from the Light realms into this dense physical reality. Perhaps the decision to remain here is not fully established for a period of time.

As was stated in an earlier answer, the dying person seems to have no aura. Possibly it goes forward to begin the process of transition to the realm of Spirit, just as in the case of birth the spiritual energy comes slowly into the physical plane, perhaps to lessen the shock of transition. This is all conjecture on my part, but it is tasty food for thought.

Q *Doesn't the aura continually change?*
A Yes and no. The health aura (that is the three inner auric bodies) changes slowly as a person's health, personality and fundamental beliefs change. The fourth auric body, called the astral auric body, is everchanging as our emotions churn and shift with the tides of thought and experience. The fifth, sixth and seventh auric bodies are much less active in appearance than the slowly-evolving health aura.

Q *Do you see auras around animals?*
A Yes, as well as trees, rocks, tables and even some scientists! Almost everything has some kind of light emanating from it. I don't really know if the light coming from an inanimate object is generated from within the object or if it is a collector of energy from outside itself. All things in the physical plane have activity on the atomic level, that is, electrons, neutrons, protons, neutrinos, quarks, etc. are very much alive and active in matter. Perhaps the emanations from 'inanimate' matter comes from this type of activity.

Animals such as domestic pets have rather simple auric bodies (two or three), often bright light blues and greens like the auras of babies.

Q *Do you see auras all the time?*
A The question implies that I spend my waking hours focused on auric emanations. It would be like asking you if you are always aware of your peripheral vision. While I am always perceiving, on some level, auric messages, I usually focus on them when it is necessary. To some degree I have had to tune out the visual imagery, but this only became a 'problem' since I found that I was able to interpret consciously what I am seeing. Before that my auric sight was just my natural way of seeing things.

We all perceive the auras of others whether we are conscious of it or not. Have you ever walked into a party where you didn't know a soul and as you walked around there were people that you just didn't like? Maybe some of them didn't fit into the range of acceptability because of their physical appearance, or because of what you could pick up from their conversation as you walked by; but many of those whom you did not like looked perfectly fine and were not saying anything that you found objectionable. You just knew that you were not interested in them, or perhaps they were even frightening 'for some reason'.

Those of us who have found ourselves making the same mistakes in our relationship choices may wonder how we could pick the same type of person each time. Some people always end up in relationships with alcoholics or people who are physically violent. They will tell you that when they first started going out with these people they had no indications that they were violent or drinkers. The truth is that we perceive these things unconsciously from each other's auras.

Why would someone purposefully set out to find people who are violent or alcoholics or destructive? Because, for reasons of past experience, or karma, those attracted to these kinds of people are 'rescuers'. Until the 'rescuer' changes his or her way of thinking he/she will continue to seek out these relationships and his/her unconscious interpretation of information from the aura will serve to help him/her find the sought-after personality every time.

As time goes on and I get more experienced in viewing the aura, I find that I am seeing more detail and more and more complex colours. When I am in consultation with a client I spend a lot of time focused in one area, say the shoulder, tuning into the various densities of energy by adjusting my consciousness to them. In this way I am able to show a lot of detail in the drawing. Looking quickly or generally at a person's aura provides much less detailed information on a conscious level but, as I have said, we are continually processing information from other's auras on an intuitive level.

2

The Double Etheric or Health Aura

We will begin now to look more closely at the auric bodies. The natural place to start is at the edge of the physical body with the first of the three inner bands or bodies of the aura.

Those who are just beginning to see auras report seeing a grey to white bluish haze extending out some 4-8 ins (10-20cm) from the body. This has been called the double etheric or health aura.

The emanations from the health aura reflect a person's physical health, fundamental motivations, and the workings of the present personality.

As I see it, there are three distinct auric bodies in the health aura: the physical auric body, the etheric auric body and the vital auric body.

The emanations in these bodies are most useful for exploring the physical health of a person. If medical personnel were trained to view and interpret these bodies, many serious diseases could be diagnosed and treated before they reached a more serious state of physical distress.

I am happy to report that often after my lectures doctors and other medical personnel will make themselves known to me and express an interest in learning more about the aura. Unfortunately, it will probably be many years before the established medical machine begins to accept the aura as a diagnostic tool and medical schools offer it as a regular part of the curriculum. At present the official word is that diagnosis by this method is considered quackery and is illegal in the United States. It is inevitable that one day the use of the aura in diagnosis will be an inseparable part of the process.

The Physical Auric Body

The observers will see a bright white or light-blue band beginning at the edge of the skin and extending out from ⅛-1½ in (3mm-3.5cm). (For beginners, it is most easily seen near the sides of the fingers.) It sometimes appears to be a colourless gap between the physical body and the coloured auric bodies. This is the Physical Auric Body.

This body is very bright and dense due to physical matter such as mucus and skin particles that are sloughed off the physical body during breathing and movement. The particles are suspended within a field of electro-magnetic energy. These particles are unique to the individual and are the means by which animals such as bloodhounds are able to discern and track down specific individuals.

In good health this auric band is bright, clear and uniform in size as it surrounds the body. In ill health this band will be seen to bulge radically near the area affected by disease or injury (see Fig. 1).

The physical auric body is where ill health can first be seen in an individual before it manifests as something able to be picked up by a physician, and often even before the individual has had any symptoms. In later stages of illness the bulging of the physical auric body will appear to disrupt the etheric auric body (causing a hole) and the vital auric body (reducing the radiance).

I have converted those who have doubted I was able to see these emanations during a reading by pointing out shoulders greatly stressed by tennis and raquetball, or old injuries that still caused problems. One woman thought for a long time after I pointed out a large disruption below her knee; she couldn't remember any injury there. Suddenly her face lit up; 'Oh yes! I was hit by a train there when I was very little.'

In a good percentage of those who come for a reading I have seen some bulging of the physical auric body in the area of the shoulders. Usually this is not a serious disruption and often signifies some muscle tension due to stuffing stress into the trapezium muscles at the upper back and neck.

One of my clients recently displayed bulging at the back of the head. I pointed out the disruptions and told her it appeared the bulging was going away. She reported that she had been hospitalized for extensive testing in that area. It seems she had been having painful headaches and the doctors could find nothing wrong. It was obvious to me that the headaches were stress related and I told her so. She said she had figured that out and had begun to use techniques to deal with her stress, the headaches have almost gone away.

One of the controversial 'proofs' of the aura's existence is Kirlian photography. It could very well be a photographic method which can depict the physical auric body.

Invented by Soviet husband and wife team Semyon and Valentina Kirlian some forty years ago, the photographic technique utilized a high-frequency spark generator and the usual film and paper to produce remarkable images of what they called bioplasmic energy.

When organic or inorganic matter is placed on the plate-electrode and the spark generator is switched on briefly, an image is formed on the film. These images look like fingerlets of sparks which are usually strongest at the perimeter of the object but also appear in patterns at the inner surface as well (see Fig. 2).

Later Soviet researchers discovered that if they placed a leaf taken from a plant on the plate-electrode, and removed half of it, the leaf appeared whole in the photograph! The energy the leaf was emitting was not affected by the amputation of part of it. This may help to explain the 'phantom leg' syndrome often experienced by amputees for varying periods of time after an arm or leg has been removed. Amputees report feeling pain, for example, in the toe of a leg that has been removed. To my way of thinking this is a pretty good indication that the human body has an energy body as well.

Dr Gustaf Stromberg, an astronomer for nearly thirty years at the Mt Wilson Observatory in Southern California, did not always have his mind on the stars. He postulated a theory that all life as we know it here on the physical plane comes from and remains rooted in the non-physical universe. He believed that energy and form emerge from this non-physical universe according to a deliberate plan of patterns of fields which govern the world we perceive. Stromberg hypothesized that such fields not only emerge from the non-physical world but return to that world at the moment which we would regard as physical death.

Researchers at Yale University headed by Drs H.S. Burr and F.S.C Northrup conducted a series of experiments to determine the validity of their own 'electro-dynamic' theory of life. Their experiments showed that all living things had a complex electrical field surrounding them that extended beyond the limits of human vision. Using an extremely sensitive device (an ultra-sensitive micro-voltmeter) which measures these electrical fields down to a millionth of a volt, Burr found that as oxygen is removed from the environment of the living organism, the surrounding electrical field begins to contract without changing in structure and disappears at the moment of death.

'It is hard to escape the conclusion,' said Burr, 'that the electrical pattern is primary and in some measure at least determines the morphological pattern.'

The experimenting and research continues in all parts of the globe and in all manner of disciplines. The deeper we delve into matter, the more we are shown that what we are perceiving as a solid tangible world is actually an illusion. Scientists have gone beyond electrons into quarks and neutrinos. The world of the tiniest particles known to man is not so much removed from the astronomical world of Gustaf Stromberg.

The Etheric Auric Body

Apparition, spirit, ghost, *Doppelgänger*, phantom — these are terms that have been used in times past to describe the etheric double (not to be confused with the double etheric). The etheric double is an etheric body which is exactly like its physical counterpart in every detail. It is the transition pattern for the physical body created out of the energy from the non-physical realm as described above in the theories of Stromberg. It is the matrix upon which the physical body exists; without this matrix the physical body begins to decay and eventually disintegrates.

At the moment of death, the etheric double and its auric emanations (the etheric auric body) carry off the Soul energy to other levels of existence in the non-physical world.

Very often those who have been declared clinically dead and were subsequently revived, report floating above their physical body, claiming they saw their body below surrounded by frantic medical personnel trying to resuscitate it. They felt that 'out of body' as they were, they still had a complete body. In fact they usually report having very little concern with the physical vehicle below them.

The 'phantom limb' phenomenon described earlier not only involves the physical auric body but the etheric double as well. As the physical auric body contracts in around the area of the stump, the etheric double decays in the area where the amputated part used to be and the feeling associated with the phantom limb disappears.

The emanations from the etheric double collect at the far edge of the physical auric body and extend out from 1-4 ins (2.5-10cm) in all directions from the body (see Fig. 1).

The early literature on the aura often combined this auric body with the next (the vital auric body), treating them as one. The literature called this combined body the double etheric auric body. The way that I see it, these two bodies are quite separate in make-up and function. The reason they are often treated as one is due to the fact that both are very bright and are usually the first auric bodies perceived by novice viewers. (I will discuss the vital auric body in detail in the next section.)

When people first begin to view the etheric auric body they often describe it as a hazy light-blue or grey smoke emanating from the body. To the more practised viewer this part of the aura will exude many different colours. I have seen orange, greens, blues, violet and even yellow.

When the etheric auric body goes into transition, I have observed an overlay of colours, for example, a transparent blue in areas over a general field of orange. Sometimes this will manifest as several colours overlaid in the case of those whose direction is not quite defined as yet.

In the diagnosis of disease the etheric auric body is important. If the disease or injury is more serious than simple muscle stress, the bulging in the physical auric body will actually push the etheric auric body out of the way, creating a hole. This is usually the stage just before a disease will show up physically. The etheric level hole will permit negative factors to enter from an active inpulling vital auric body which will most often lead to more serious illness if it is not treated. Sometimes the etheric auric body resists being pushed out of the way and will appear to bulge along with the physical auric body. This indicates a person who has good resistance to serious illness. In these cases the disease or injury will usually manifest less seriously and will heal or repair itself much more quickly than in those whose resistance has allowed a hole to be created.

The etheric auric body is an indicator of what is happening at very fundamental levels of a person's being. What is the underlying basis of this person's actions at this time? Is this person choosing a growth mode? a balancing mode? Is he acting out his life in a strictly intuitive way? Is she acting out her life from anger? All of these questions can be answered by the analysis of the colour or colours in this auric body.

One of the most fascinating aspects of the etheric auric body is its use, by physical or materializing mediums, to produce visual phenomena. When calling on spiritual entities to materialize in the physical plane, these mediums draw from the dense particles of their etheric aura to create a substance called ectoplasm. Ectoplasm, which has been witnessed by thousands of people and photographed hundreds of times, can be seen pouring out of the stomachs, ears, noses and mouths of mediums in trance. The ectoplasm takes on the form dictated by the spiritual entity that has been called.

I have seen estoplasm around mediums in trance and have even had the good fortune of momentarily seeing it form into a face but this has only occurred three times in the hundreds of aura portraits that I have done in the past years.

The first time I saw this phenomenon was my favourite. I was doing the portrait of a particularly powerful medium in Denver and suddenly a blue smokey face appeared above her head. Then, just as quickly, it faded. Mentally I asked it to reappear so tht I could draw it onto the portrait. The face did not reappear; instead, a voice in my head said to take my light-blue pencil, touch the point to the paper and move it back and forth in horizontal lines until the face was drawn. I did what the voice said and a man's face was drawn, much the same as a computer would print out a picture one line at a time. When I showed the picture to the medium she said it was a great likeness of her ex-husband.

The Vital Auric Body

Beginning at the outer of the etheric auric body and extending from 2-6ins (5-16cms) (sometimes as far as 12ins (30cms)) the observer will find a very bright body made up of radiant fingerlets of lines of energy extending out in all directions. The vital auric body is unique in that not only does it radiate outward; it also draws energy inward. This body pulls vital energy from the sun and our surrounding environment, sends it into the physical body and nourishes it.

In diagnosing the severity with which an illness has affected an area, the vital auric body is very helpful. Areas of disruption due to disease or illness are drained of vital energy. This causes the normally straight radiant lines of energy to droop, eventually falling to the innermost portion of this auric body in an often chaotic and matted fashion much like the wet fur of a long-haired animal. The matting of these radiant lines not only shows a lesser degree of energy getting into the area of the physical body, but also actually inhibits the energy flow at that point. Without an incoming continuous flow of vital energy, the tissues will begin to decay or atrophy.

As was noted earlier, in serious cases of auric disruption the physical auric body will bulge into the etheric auric body, often causing a hole. This hole then affects the vital auric body, causing the drooping of the radiant lines (see Fig. 1).

The vital auric body touches the astral or emotional auric body (see Chapter 3), and expands into it at times of high vitality. This is an important relationship because the vital auric body also acts to absorb emotional disruptions, pulling them into the inner layers of the aura and sending them for processing to the appropriate chakra (see p. 49) or energy vortex. Each chakra deals with a specific kind of energy. For example, another person's resentment aimed at you can become lodged in the astral auric body where, if it is not dealt with, it will be drawn in by the vital auric body, and diminish vitality. The vital auric body then passes this negative energy on to the second, third and fourth chakras where it is lodged in the nearby organs, in this case the heart, stomach, liver and intestinal tract. This negative energy may begin as simple gas or intestinal cramps or indigestion on the physical plane and, if not heeded, could eventually manifest as serious organ malfunction or even cancer. When emotional disruptions are ignored or 'stuffed' they have to manifest on the physical plane to get our attention. We would all be better off if we dealt with our anger and resentments and other emotional issues before they manifested as sickness or death.

When our vitality is reduced we feel rundown and tired. This will appear as a great reduction in the size of the vital auric body, which will sometimes shrink down to ½ in (1.2cms). Its brightness dims and makes it difficult to see. This is what this auric body looks like when, in medical terms, your resistance is low and disease has a chance to enter your physical system.

Because of its proximity to and interrelationship with the emotional body, the vital auric body is a good indicator of what is occurring in the area of personality. The radiant lines of this body go out to the minds of others, picking up their personality and at the same time leaving other people with an impression of your personality or charisma.

Colours are significant for further examination of health and personality matters.

Tone, brightness, clarity and other factors enter into the analysis. This will be discussed in depth in chapter 6.

It is important to remember that the physical, etheric and vital auric bodies are very resilient. Just like the physical body, the auric bodies can take many years of constant abuse before becoming permanently disrupted.

Contrary to the belief of some, the aura does recover from drug abuse and disease. With time and treatment the aura most often will recuperate, and may become even better than it was before the abuses and/or disease. When I speak of treatment, I mean healing not only the physical problem, but the auric disruptions and the emotional and intellectual causes as well. (I will discuss more about healing in Chapter 8.)

3

The Thought Plane Aura

In the previous chapter we discussed the three auric bands that emanate from the three denser bodies of the human animal. These inner bands or layers (the health aura) are important in diagnosing physical health. Just as important in diagnosis are the next two auric bodies, which exhibit elements that are present within the emotional and mental health of a person.

The inner layers of the aura are quite dense in composition compared with the more subtle structure of the outer layers and therefore more difficult to see, even by a well-practised metaphysician. As I adjust my inner self to tune into these subtle layers I have to watch carefully because I often get only fleeting glimpses of them. But what impressive glimpses they are!

The Astral Auric Body

The first of these bodies is the astral auric body. It is usually the largest of the lower auric bodies and creates the ovoid shape usually associated with the aura.

I have observed this part of the aura to be anywhere from 4 ins (10cms) to several feet wide. Usually, however, it is approximately 2 ft (60cms) wide, extending from the outer edge of the vital auric body (see Fig. 3).

The astral auric body is created from the emanations from the astral body which is where we store our complete past and present life history. We draw upon this information as needed in our current lives to further our evolvement as spiritual beings.

The existence of this auric body has been disputed among metaphysicians throughout time because of its subtle and rather philosophical nature. Whereas there are thousands of people who are aware that they are able to see some form or part of the denser layers of the inner auric bodies, there are considerably fewer people who actually observe the astral auric body. Most of those metaphysicians who work with the astral aura 'see' it only with their Inner Eye or psychic/intuitive sense. I see this auric body with my eyes but I also call upon my Inner Eye for clarification and confirmation of information that may not totally form in my mind as the images pass through my vision. In that way the information I give to a client is amplified and verified and I can deliver it with confidence.

Though they are rare, there are exceptions to this subtlety of vision when viewing this auric body. Sometimes the astral auric body will appear to me to be even brighter than some parts of the inner aura. This occurs primarily with clients who are completely open with their emotions during our session. They are ready to work on themselves and consequently display everything to me. Many people, however, are 'masked', hiding their true feelings for fear that others will see the 'horrible reality' of who they really are. The truth is we all have parts of ourselves that we don't like. It is important to open up our emotional selves and share who we are with others; by doing so we find that our deep-dark selves are actually not so bad after all.

The astral auric body is often the first place where the experiences of 'good' or 'bad' create an effect. For example, you are driving down a crowded highway. The traffic is moving at a snail's pace and you are forced to move along slower and slower because of a garbage truck in front of you. The traffic in the oncoming lane is steady, offering you no chance to pass. Behind you is a new red sports car. Its driver is impatient to overtake. He pulls up close behind you and your reaction is to want to pass the truck quickly, just to get away from this maniac. But the truck is wide and it is difficult to see just when a break in oncoming traffic will occur. The driver of the sports car begins to blast away on his horn. He moves even closer to your rear bumper. Your heart begins to race. Your mind is searching for a solution. The man in the sports car begins hollering out of his window at you. You begin to feel an aching in your stomach. (Your second chakra, the energy centre located near the navel, has already begun to process the thought forms that have knifed their way to you from the being in the red sports car.) Because of past judgements formed around previous experiences in your subconscious mind you have decided to label this experience as negative.

The physical symptom created is pain in the stomach. It is a warning to the brain that something is wrong and needs immediate attention. The physical causes of the pain are an excess amount of acid being generated in the stomach as well as a surge of adrenalin and numerous other chemicals all being created to get the attention of the brain which is preoccupied with the dilemma of how to deal with the sports car.

The 'negative' energy is immediately sent on to the astral body where its effects can be seen in emanations of the astral auric body. Since all experiences are stored in the astral body these new experiences seek out like ones which compound old images or beliefs about yourself such as 'I'm such a coward' or 'I am terribly inept behind the wheel'.

In this example, disruptions form in the astral auric body around the area of the stomach. These disruptions usually become what we who see auras would call 'thought-forms', usually ugly, sharp-edged, muddy-coloured things, anywhere from the size of a small seed to the size of a large grapefruit. This thought-form, strengthened by similar beliefs gathered in the astral body, begins to irritate the radiant lines of the vital auric body causing them to diminish in size and eventually to lay down giving the appearance of wet fur (see Fig. 1). With the vital auric body weakened in this way an opening is created for the thought-form to being to attack the etheric auric body which, of course, directly affects the etheric body, the very framework upon which life on this physical plane exists. At this point the brain is signalled to release the acids and other chemicals into the area of the stomach. The whole process occurred in less time than it took for the red sports-car driver to honk his horn.

This same process can enter your system from any of the other energy centres as well. Often two or three centres are affected during a single experience. In this case, your heart chakra is also affected. The heart chakra, located just right of your physical heart in the centre of your chest, is where information regarding your relationships with the external world is processed. It is also the centre where you process your own self-love, or lack of it. The heart chakra has taken in the information being sent from the situation with the red sports car. It comes in without judgement and is distributed to the subconscious mind which labels it according to the judgements surrounding past experiences. Again the label is a 'negative' one. You begin to take the experience personally, such as 'It's really me the driver hates', and you become more emotionally distressed. Old thought-forms and beliefs gather in the astral auric body causing a ring of disruption around the body in the area of the heart chakra and your heart begins to pound and ache.

Your third chakra, located in the solar plexus (where your ribs come together at the diaphragm), is also affected in this situation. This energy centre is where the distribution of your personal power occurs. A disruption at this point could cause you to feel helpless or powerless to deal with this situation in any way or it could trigger a feeling that you do not have the resources to deal with the situation. In this case, however, the subconscious mind does not have sufficient strength reserves because of its current belief systems and decides to label this experience as 'negative' and again like thought-forms gather to cause more disruption in the astral auric body and so on.

With so many blockages occurring on so many levels in the emotional body, the lower mental body, and its auric counterpart the lower mental auric body, are affected and your judgement becomes clouded and faulty. In a panic you pull out into oncoming traffic. An oncoming car swerves to avoid you and ends up in a farmer's field on its side. Reacting wildly, you pull back into your place behind the garbage truck. Unfortunately, the red sports car has taken that space and you collide. The two of you meet in 'Heaven' and discuss how you both could have processed things a little better in that lifetime.

Some people carry around active 'negative' thought-forms for a considerable amount of time. These thought forms can remain active within the astral auric body for a brief moment, many years, or even several lifetimes. The longer that these disruptors are allowed to stay in the astral auric body, the larger they grow and the stronger they become and the more damage is done to physical and emotional systems. This is not to say that 'negative' thought-forms are unnatural or 'bad'. On the contrary they serve us well, for when an important lesson is to be learned by our Essence Self it is sometimes only the build-up of these thought forms, and the physical and emotional destruction created, that demands our attention so that we can deal with the root of the problem and continue to evolve.

I recently did a consultation for a man whose astral auric body was so disrupted in the area of his stomach (second and third chakras) I could actually feel the pain in my stomach. I knew if I were to reach over and gently poke him in that area he would experience severe pain. On examining his astral auric body I discovered 'negative' thought-forms lodged there that appeared to be long-lived and quite powerful.

The result of having these thought forms near the third chakra was a feeling of powerlessness in most aspects of his life. He had developed a poor self-image and felt emotionally distraught and impotent (second chakra). To compensate for the aching feeling in his gut he would over-eat. This would relieve the physical feeling for a while as the food was being digested but soon the 'empty' feeling would return and he would run to the refrigerator once again. Eventually he had built up quite a large layer of fat on his belly to protect these chakras. The fatter he got, the more powerless he felt and his self-esteem fell to rock bottom. I am happy to say that by examining the root of his problems and finding an understanding of who he 'really' is the man has begun to reverse this process and is returning to a healthier, more power-filled life. The thought forms, though still present, are greatly reduced in size and strength. My client used body fat to insulate and protect his second and third chakras with disastrous results. There are better ways to protect these important centres which I will discuss in chapter 5.

In ideal emotional health the astral auric body appears to me as a bright, clear sky-blue, sometimes slightly churning like blue smoke in a gentle breeze. I have noted that those who exhibit this ideal emotional state actually transmit transquillity to those around them.

For instance, two friends are sitting side by side. One is exhibiting a degree of emotional stress stimulated by an argument with her mother. The astral auric body of the other is displaying the beautiful sky-blue of an ideal emotional state. The distressed aura is churning wildly with the colours orange, dark green and flecks of bright red. As the friends start talking, the peaceful blue begins to seep into the distressed auric body causing, temporarily, a calming effect.

Given time, both the astral and lower mental auric bodies of an individual will join with those around him or her in most circusmtances. Those who are empathic or extremely sensitive to the moods of others will find that they pick up the predominant feeling almost immediately. Happiness, fear, anger and depression can be extremely infectious.

For example, as a student in Boston in the late 1960s I had gone to the Commons (a large tree-filled park in the heart of the city) for a relaxing walk in the warm sun. The 60s were difficult times for young American men. The war in Vietnam was winding ever on, young men were being drafted and sent off to the war in large numbers. Most of us didn't have the slightest idea of what we were fighting and dying for. The anti-war movement was growing strong in the USA. It was especially strong in Boston, where the students of various universities and colleges practically outnumber the full-time residents for a major portion of the year. Students were the lifeblood of the peace movement.

So it was, on this beautiful sunny day, the Commons was host to an anti-war demonstration. At that time in my life I was not very interested in politics. I was interested in peace but this angry demonstration didn't seem to have anything even remotely to do with peace. Since I always enjoy a little street theatre, I casually wandered over to the large crowd to be entertained.

As I got closer to the crowd I began to feel the anger that was being generated there. In just a few short moments I, too, was becoming angry. I had scarcely had a chance to get involved in what the speaker was saying. Later I realized that the further away from the mob I got, the less angry I felt until, at the other side of the Commons, I was once again able to enjoy the sunshine and trees. But the experience had left its impression and stimulated my intellect (a thought form had lodged itself neatly at the borders of the astral auric body and the lower mental auric body) regarding my place in a political world. The thought form generated that day had a strong effect on me for many years. Also it was the day I learned to associate the colour red with anger. Even though it would be some years before I would understand that what I had been seeing were auras, I knew on some level that the sea of red I had so casually walked into was actually the blending together of the astral auric bodies of all those gathered there. Consider the old expression 'the angry mob saw red'.

This astral auric body blending effect occurs in almost all gatherings of three or more people. I say three or more because in the case of two people there is still a chance that the strength of the individual ego will deny a blending. Simply add a third person and the ego is forced to concentrate on dealing with two beings and the power is divided into half for each individual. The need then is to join emotionally, a need that offers the best possibility for survival in a social sense. We have all seen how many people have to know what the rest of their social group is going to do before they make their decision as to how they will respond. The same occurs on the emotional level.

Of course there are various levels of emotional power and in the cases of stress, sadness, depression and joy there is a great deal of power being generated. We have all found ourselves caught up in someone else's emotions from time to time. Do you live with a spouse who is habitually angry or depressed? How does it affect your attitudes and feelings? Wouldn't it be wonderful to be around happy, positive people instead? How would that affect your attitudes? How do your feelings affect those around you? What are you projecting to the astral auric bodies of others?

Our emotions and those of others can become another important form of environmental pollution, or they can be a form of life-enhancing, world-changing positive energy.

Perhaps in this world of rapid communication we are doing great harm to our health by listening to what our news journalists have chosen to feed us via television and the other forms of news. Computer technicians have an expression 'garbage in. . .garbage out'. Choosing to focus on the positive in your life can affect your health and the health of those around you in a positive way. Focusing on the opposite will bring the opposite result. If it is true for the physical body that 'we are what we eat' then perhaps we ought to consider seriously our 'food for thought' for healthier mental and emotional bodies.

When I perceive anger in the astral auric body it usually appears to be small angular chips of intense red. Often these chips are observed near the heart chakra where they interfere with the free flow of energy being processed there. Anger lodged in this area manifests outwardly as 'coldness' or 'hardness' of attitude. People who 'stuff their anger', as it is often called, appear to be aloof and unapproachable, often displaying an attitude of superiority masking their true feelings of inadequacy and vulnerability. Maintaining a hard exterior repels other people and thus, to their way of thinking, they reduce their chances of ever being hurt by others. In reality they hurt themselves with isolation and anger more than any other being could ever do.

Depression in the astral auric body appears to me as misty black clouds of varying densities depending upon the degree of affliction. The black mist will vary in appearance from small and spotty (the size of grapes) to a large mass (taking up to one third of this auric body). The former represents natural depression, that which can occur within the parameters of life's everyday problems. This type of depression usually is short-lived and does not interfere with an individual's ability to function normally on a daily basis. The latter represents a more severe type of depression where an individual's ability to function on a daily basis is greatly interrupted. This deep form of depression may not always be exclusively connected to the condition of the astral body but is often organic in nature. In the case of organically caused depression the diagnostician will find jagged disruptions of all sizes in the physical, etheric, and vital auric bodies, usually in one of the quadrants near the head.

I have never seen a completely black astral auric body although others have reported seeing such a phenomenon. I would hypothesize that the astral auric body would appear that way just prior to a 'successful' suicide. However, as stated earlier, one would probably not see any aura at that point due to the radically diminished auric energy prior to impending death.

Sadness, which is often associated with depression, looks to me like thin, wispy black or grey smoke, much the same as the smoke that is given off by a stick of incense. It usually appears to be rising up from the area in the astral auric body directly across from the lower major chakras, the centres for the processing and distributing of emotional energy base power, and personal power. When the wispy smoke appears near the area of the head without seeming to be rooted in the lower chakras it usually indicates someone who has an overconcern or out-of-control compassion for world events or for certain groups of people, such as family members.

On the positive side, I see orange waves or strata of energy indicating a balancing or harmonizing factor in the astral auric body. This orange factor is generated to help us to deal with past or current depression, anger or sadness. It is created by an effort, either conscious or subconscious, to deal with old thought-forms lodged within the emotional field. The colour, rather than actually being the effect, is the visual manifestation of the process in effect, as are all of the colours in the aura.

Some other positive indicators are the general brightness and clarity of colour, as well as the presence of such colours as a pine-needle green, a grass green, magenta, pink or apricot, and many others. I will deal with the meaning of colour in the aura in Chapter 6.

The Lower Mental Auric Body

The second part of the thought plane aura is also the last of the five lower auric bodies. It is called the lower mental auric body. The name may sound a bit uncomplimentary. Often when I am interpreting a person's aura and I come to the lower mental auric body people think I am telling them that they have a low mentality. Actually the name delineates a difference between everyday conscious thought (lower mental) and the Higher Mind (higher mental auric body) which expresses thought on other than a mundane or everyday level. The lower mental auric body shows a person's abilities on the conscious or intellectual level.

In a person who has a good command of his or her intellectual abilities this auric band is bright and wide (usually from 1½-8 ins (4-20cms) wide, especially in the region of the head). This band almost always appears to be clear, bright yellow in the case of good mental health, pulsing outward from the somewhat indistinct edge of the astral auric body.

The lower mental auric body is often confused with the astral auric body because they actually share the same large ovoid space. Only when the mind is very active or when conscious thought can be separated from the emotions can the yellow pulsing be seen outside the boundaries of the astral auric body. Our everyday thinking and our emotions are so interlinked that it makes it difficult for the uninitiated to separate them for analysis.

In the auras of children (aged one to ten years) I have observed that the more easily seen of the two auric bodies is the pulsing yellow lower mental auric body. It occupies the area that is most often the astral auric body in adults. Children, as a survival mechanism, use intellectual manipulation as a primary force to supply their needs. This is not to say that children do not have an emotional side, they do, but tears and screaming do not always betray true emotions; they are often devices that bring quick results from those entrusted with the care of children. Some of us still use the 'it's the squeaky wheel that gets greased' device as adults.

After the age of ten years or so the emotional side of our nature becomes more activated and takes on a more important role in our everyday life. As puberty ensues, a surging, seemingly out-of-control emotional state surrounds us and hormonal changes are dramatic. A child begins to view the world with a different rationale. In this transition period the child will still use the old manipulative techniques to get what he wants but he will now be aware of what his actions create and how they affect the emotions of his parents. This is a period of testing and experimentation. Parents must be aware of what is happening. Most often they will react to their child's behaviour in much the same way as they have done for the past ten or twelve years. This is a mistake because the child has changed and so must the parent. To become very strict or authoritarian at this point in the game means certain failure. It is a time to give the child some 'rein' and allow him to suffer the unpleasant consequences (within limits) or rewards of his own actions. He is testing out his new-found adulthood and to insist he remain a child is fruitless. A parent must trust that all that he or she has done in the primary years has served to create a being who will be prepared to make the right choices in this transition period. The role of the parent must shift from one of authority to that of a guide or counsellor.

Aurically, the intense initial emotional surges gradually move into a more balanced state. In time they level out to create a harmony between emotions and intellect (usually by the thirtieth year) although there are a few cases in which this balance is never achieved. Most of us swing back and forth on an ever-slowing pendulum, eventually seeking a reasonably stable balance of thought and emotion. Others of us cling to the intellect and deny the emotional side of our nature.

In observing the lower mental auric body I have noted red flecks representing anger can be found in this auric field apart from the astral auric body. These flecks generated in the emotional body enter the area of conscious thought and obstruct the processes occurring there. I have also seen the black clouds of depression there causing obstructions and making 'clear thinking' very difficult. Often when a client is working on some all-encompassing problem in his life I will observe a dark orange wedge at the upper edge of the lower mental auric body above the head. This orange indicates a 'sorting out' and a harmonizing process, trying to clear out blockages to the flow of higher energy into the chakra system, which is continually entering at the crown of the head. Therefore, not only do difficult problems create trouble in the dense physical world but they also inhibit the natural flow of the much needed higher energies which are necessary to help solve the problem in the first place.

Although there are as many forms of mental illness as there are mentally-ill individuals, the predominant feature in the auras of these people is a dramatic lack of symmetry in the overall ovoid shape of the aura (see Fig. 4). That is, one quadrant or another will be quite different in size from the others. Sometimes one half of the auric field can be very wide and extended while the other half appears to be thin and shrivelled. At other times one side can be muddied and dark with the other side clear and bright. At one moment the extended side will be reaching out beyond the limits of an 'average' aura and in the next instant it can snap back and become shrivelled. Conversely, the shrivelled side can puff out to many times its original size. This radical changing and assymmetry is brightest and most easily observed near the area of the head and shoulders.

Another important visual feature of mental illness is the creation of polyps of astral and lower mental auric energy which grow rapidly out and away from the auric bodies. These polyps (which look somewhat like dripping candle wax) will fly out and away from the auric field with the speed of an attacking bird.

For those who are empathic, being in the presence of, say, a schizophrenic who is experiencing an episode of intense personality distortion can be a harrowing experience. The outpouring of this intense energy can be as overwhelming to feel as it is to see.

I have had occasion to see many types of convulsive seizures during my years of work in an institution for the mentally-disabled. Grand mal seizures, which many victims of epilepsy endure, exhibit an incredible outpouring of sharp white-blue lines that could be likened to sparks flying off a grinding wheel when a metal implement is being sharpened.

A seizure of the grand mal variety can actually affect the thinking and emotional fields of those in close proximity to the victim. I have often felt the electrical 'sparking' in my physical body. It could be likened to the sensation one would get from holding a lighted sparkler near one's face — an intermittent stinging of tiny, hot projectiles. After the seizure, I, like the victim of the episode, would feel drained and tired.

When diagnosing the state of mental health in an individual it is important to consider the whole aura. If mental illness of some kind appears to be present it would be wise to have a closer look to see if there are any disruptions in the inner layers of the auric field. If bulging or sharp disruptions appear in any quadrant around the head in the physical, etheric, and or vital auric bodies an organic cause may be indicated, such as a tumor in the brain or some kind of head injury. One must always be aware of the totality of the human aura when diagnosing both physical and mental health. A qualified physician trained to observe auric emanations would be far ahead of the game in helping to treat the myriad of physical and mental diseases that plague the human being. Perhaps one day when the limits imposed by the medical hierarchy's prejudices toward the use of the aura in diagnosis are eliminated we will be allowed to experience the optimum in health care.

4

The Higher Auric Bodies

One of the most unique aspects of the human aura is its division into two separate, equally sized bodies of energy. I am not speaking here of the divisions within each body we discussed earlier, but about two distinct and separate forms, each ovoid in shape — one surrounding the physical body and the other hovering above the first (see Fig. 3).

The former, called the lower auric bodies, consists of the five layers that we have just discussed in Chapters 2 and 3. The latter consists of only two layers. It can be observed from just a few inches above the head to 50 ft (15m) above the subject.

The determining factor in the location of the higher auric bodies is the ability of the subject to draw upon and utilize the powerful energies contained within these bodies. For example, a person who has very little concern for his spiritual life, his planet and his fellow beings, will be drawing down very little of the powerful energy stored in the higher auric bodies. Consequently, the higher aura will hover at some distance from the lower aura. On the other hand, a rapidly-evolving individual, one who respects his planet and all forms of life on it, will, by his need for greater quantities of higher energy, pull the higher auric bodies closer to the lower auric bodies.

The separation of these two auras is caused by the physical body's inability to withstand the power and intensity of the higher Energies. It takes many lifetimes or incarnations of learning and evolvement to be able to increase the ability of the physical body to accommodate this spiritual energy.

Those who have been able to pull the higher aura down into the lower aura for sustained periods of time or even a complete lifetime have been given various titles throughout the history of mankind: saint, buddha, prophet, sage, enlightened one, guru, master, christ.

Throughout my investigations of people's auras there have been many who have had their higher aura situated very near the lower aura. Only twice have I seen the two auras intersecting, that is, the higher aura sharing a few inches of its mass with a few inches of the top part of the lower aura. It appeared that the two bodies were beginning to merge to become one.

One such person is a very famous author, lecturer and educator whose dynamic lectures on the subject of love inspire all who attend his sell-out performances. Dr Leo Buscaglia explodes with an enthusiasm that is infectious. Everywhere he goes he motivates thousands to grow and evolve more positively by helping them to understand the importance of expressing love in all aspects of their lives.

I had the great fortune to attend one of Dr Buscaglia's lectures in Denver some years ago. The hall was filled to capacity, some 6000 people. Even though my seat was located many rows back from the stage I was able to see Dr Buscaglia's immense and brightly glowing aura quite well.

It is his custom to stay after his lecture and give hugs to any and all who wish to have one. This particular evening over half of the audience stayed to receive their hug. It was almost two hours before it was my turn. As I approached this man I could see that his higher aura was intersecting with the lower. The outermost portion of the lower aura (the lower mental auric body) was growing up around the higher mental auric body (the outermost layer of the higher aura).

The other person is a retired doctor in his late sixties. A very gentle and deeply compassionate man, he had given up his practice in Arizona to devote his time to healing by sending energies through his hands and various chakras. As I talked with him I could see little tears welling up in his eyes as he connected himself to me empathically. It was as if he were becoming me for a time to diagnose my mental, physical and emotional health.

This doctor happily agreed to allow me to draw his aura. The drawing showed the intersection of his higher and lower auras — the bright, pulsing yellow of the lower mental auric body growing up along the outer edges of the higher mental auric body. The two auras were becoming one auric body. When this process is complete, probably in this lifetime for these two special men, there will be no need to incarnate into another physical lifetime. These entities will move on up the evolutionary ladder in spiritual form, ultimately returning to the Source.

The Higher Mental Auric Body

The external edge of the higher aura is usually violet in colour with a layer of dark blue at its innermost part. Because of the intense energy of this body it vibrates at a frequency that is difficult to see with the physical eye. Only a portion of this body is visible to me, appearing in cross-section as a wide crescent shape, usually 24 ins (60cms) from side to side.

The higher mental auric body contains the energies which supply us with our higher mind functioning capabilities. It is our intellectual link with our Source. This is the place where our higher self dwells, supplying information of a broader nature than our brain creates from daily experiences. Also located here is the sum total of Universal Knowledge, our own tap into the great data bank of the universe. It is this body that psychics use to provide information of an esoteric nature to their clients.

In the case of a medium who channels beings on other levels of vibration, this auric body acts to translate formless information into concrete messages that can be processed by the lower mental auric body.

By observing the 'crescent's' movement I have been able to tell whether a medium is actually channelling or not. In a genuine channelling the 'crescent' moves rapidly down from its normal position. As it gets closer to the top of the head it appears to shrink to half of its original size, brightening in intensity. At this point the medium is breathing deeply, focusing on 'getting out of the way' of the incoming information. When this has been satisfactorily accomplished the 'crescent' touches the top of the medium's head. Suddenly the medium's multicoloured, multilayered aura flashes into one solid, violet-coloured body. In some cases I have watched as the medium's aura changed in size as well, as if a very large being was present.

I once got into trouble with my metaphysical study group for walking out in the middle of a so-called trance session. It was obvious to me that the 'medium' was merely there for our money. Perhaps he was able to tap into higher energies from time to time but he wasn't doing it that evening and he was unwilling to admit it to us. Instead, he sat there pretending to be delivering messages of great importance to us from another plane. Perhaps his messages were just as valid as if they had come from a higher source, but to me he was simply making fools of us all.

As I tried to leave the session quietly, I was followed by several friends who wanted to know why I was leaving. I told them that the man was not trance channelling and I couldn't sit there any longer and listen to it. They tried to humour me and even went so far as to suggest that I was leaving because the content of the message was stirring up things in me that I didn't want to deal with. They returned to the session and I went home. Several weeks later I was vindicated for my 'rudeness'; the bogus medium was exposed as a fraud by several nationally respected psychics. It seems that he and a partner had even stolen a good sum of money from their organization.

In analyzing an aura, the 'crescent' is important in that it shows the ability of the subject to use higher energies and the degree of spiritual evolvement, or the potential to evolve, that is present.

The Spiritual Auric Body

Contained within the outer layer (higher mental auric body) is the core of the higher aura. It is called the spiritual auric body. It has been described as an unimaginable, radiant, mother-of-pearl white light. I have never seen this auric body with my physical eyes, but my Inner Eye tells me that it is encased in a protective blazing gold shell.

I like to refer to this body as the 'extension cord to God', or to the Source. It is here that the highest form of energy is manifested in the physical realm.

All of the cosmic energy that we use in our earthly life is drawn from this location. Very rarely do we use it at full strength; it is usually processed as it enters the chakra system at the crown chakra. Here the pure energy is transformed into components of specific energy needed to supply our needs at the time and then it is distributed throughout the chakra system. The energy feeds the seven subtle bodies and is then sent on out into the various layers of the lower aura.

Because of the processing of pure energy at the crown chakra we are not overwhelmed by the intense properties of the energy but use it in the most efficient way.

It is because we live in such a dense and slowly vibrating realm that the spiritual auric body needs to be separated from the lower bodies which are mainly concerned with the dense activities of daily living. It is important though to remember that the higher aura is nearby and that we can consciously draw from it to continue the all-important process of our evolution.

5

Other Elements Present in the Auric Fields

Often when people look at the drawing I have made of their aura, the first thing they see is not the auric layers but rather the multicoloured bars of light cutting through it or the colourful balls of light or the odd shapes hovering all about. They comment that their aura looks like a Hollywood premiere. In this chapter we will discuss these important elements.

Energy Coming In — The Rays

Inevitably, the first question asked regarding an aura drawing is, 'What are those bars of colour next to my shoulder, head, neck, etc.? What do they mean?'

These 'bars of light' are helping energy coming from an external source. They enter from outside the aura and feed chakras that are in need of various kinds of energy. The kind of helping energy can be interpreted by examining the colours found in them.

On some level of our consciousness we make an agreement with the sender of these special energies to take them in to supply our needs. These energies or 'rays' can come from several sources. They are sent (consciously or unconsciously) from friends, teachers, mates or other people who care about us. They can also come from entities that exist on other vibrational levels. Finally, they can be sent from those beings that we have known in this or other lifetimes, beings that have since passed out of the physical realm at death.

Several years ago I was doing an aura portrait of a rather rotund, feisty old grandmother in her early seventies. While I observe and draw in the auric layers I am absorbed in what I am seeing and I am lost in inner conversation with guides and other energies who explain to me in detail the things that I am seeing. Before this part of the process I explain to my subject that it will be best if we do not talk until I am through. I usually suggest that subjects meditate (if they are meditators) or I suggest daydreaming or even taking a little nap. The woman opted to nap. Her daughter sat nearby watching silently.

After fifteen minutes had passed I had reached a place where I needed to see the rays. I asked the guides to brighten them so that I could better make out the colours. A ray appeared at the left side of the woman. It shimmered with a bright violet light, a refreshing green bar appeared next to it, both brightening. The ray was wide and straight, tapering in as it sent its healing energies pouring down into her heart chakra.

I began sketching in the ray with my violet pencil when a faint voice in my head said, 'Tell the old bag I'm waiting for her'.

I continued working on the drawing, ignoring the voice, but it was persistent; 'Tell the old bag I'm waiting for her'. It kept repeating the message until it was overriding all of my thoughts and the voices of the guides. At last, unable to concentrate enough to even see the aura, I gave in to it.

The old woman was sleeping peacefully. I took a deep breath and carefully asked her to wake up. She stirred a bit and then asked if the portrait was done. I shook my head and nervously explained that there was a voice in my head saying, 'Tell the old . . .' my voice broke 'bag. . .I'm waiting for her'.

There was a long pause. The woman's face turned pale, her jaw dropped and she began to cry. Her daughter joined in. I was convinced that I was in the wrong business.

Finally the old woman smiled. Wiping back the tears, she explained, 'That's what my husband would have said!'

Her husband had died almost three years earlier. His way of being affectionate was to use these otherwise unflattering terms to address or refer to his wife. When the woman had heard me speak the words again she knew that they were coming from him. I felt a chill, goose bumps covered my arms and we all cried.

Because this occurred while I was drawing the ray I have to assume that these rays can come from those who have passed on as well as from the worldly and other worldly beings in our lives. This particular ray was, as I have said earlier, a healing ray. It was composed of the healing and growthful 'grass' green, backed up by a shaft of violet representing a powerful and protective spiritual element. This colour combination represents one of the most powerful healing processes in the aura.

I don't often know the source of these rays but by noting their position, size, shape and colour(s) one can provide a great deal of information regarding the kinds of help that the subject is receiving.

Sometimes a ray will appear to be thin and wispy, meandering lazily away from the subject, often piercing only two or three of the outer layers of the lower aura. These are rays that are not yet established. The subject, although having agreed to accept the rays on some level, is not yet drawing on them.

On occasion I will see rays that are quite large, denoting that they have been drawn upon regularly, but which now appear to be meandering away from the body. This indicates that the rays are not being drawn upon at present. Usually the subject is avoiding some aspect of his or her life. By noting the chakra that the end of the ray is nearest to, one can analyze the root of the avoidance.

When a ray is being drawn upon it brightens, straightens out and, over time, becomes very wide.

We all have several of these helping rays working with us. I have seen very few people who have had no rays. These energies, provided from external sources, are vital to our evolvement and well-being (see Fig. 5).

Guide Energies

When most students of metaphysics think of guides or teachers they bring to mind personalized beings such as American Indians, Hindu masters, ancient Chinese sages, etc. While these entities may very well be involved in the business of our evolvement, working from their plane of existence, I have never seen Indians, Chinese or Hindus floating around in anyone's aura. Rather, I see concentric spheres of light which give off brilliant colours.

I must qualify the above statement by saying that I have, over the years, seen three faces display themselves in the aura. These displays were extremely brief and none of the faces was exotic in appearance. They were all human faces of contemporary origin; one of them, drawn into a woman's aura portrait, was later identified by the woman as her ex-husband who was alive and well on the physical plane. I believe that in those three cases, out of the hundreds of aura portraits I have drawn over the years, the face appeared because the subject needed to see a personalized being.

These concentric spheres of light are positive entity energies which have been given permission by the host Being to enter its aura for the purpose of supplying needed external energies. As with the rays, this permission is usually given on the unconscious level but can also be given on the conscious level, as in the case of prayer.

By analyzing the colours contained within the spheres and their location in the aura, we can determine what kind of helping energy is being supplied and what layer or layers of the aura are being affected. By noting the location of the nearest chakras and understanding the function of each of the chakras, we can determine the root of the disruption that has brought the guide energy in to help.

Guide energies usually display very little personality. Most of them seem to be more of a process than a personality. When I ask to see them while doing a portrait, I often get the feeling that it is an intrusion, I feel as though they are saying, 'OK, ok, let's get this aura portrait stuff over with so we can get back to something important.'

Sometimes, however, a guide energy will provide a tremendous show for me. Once, one exploded into a beautiful shimmering silver starburst; others have flip-flopped all over the aura in the shape of tear drops chasing after their tails; some have sent me overwhelming feelings of joy; and still others have covered me in warm waves of loving energy. Guide energies can give the impression of being predominantly male or female, but most seem to have no specific sexual identity. Some seem to give off an 'aura' of great wisdom while others seem full of humour, even mischievous. By and large though, guide energies exhibit a hard-working 'drone-like' energy.

Every one of us has several of these energies working within our systems for our evolvement, providing helping energies with our permission. They do not control what we do, they do not tell us what to do, although information of that sort can be brought into consciousness through the higher mental auric body by way of the lower mental auric body, if it is needed. If this should occur it is only by way of suggestion, it is not a directive. The sole function of these guides is to make available limitless helping energies that we can choose to draw into our systems. It is solely up to us whether we use them or not.

Thought Forms

Earlier we discussed how thought-forms can act to disrupt the emotional or astral auric body, eventually causing harm to the physical body. These 'negative' thought-forms come in many forms and can even manifest as symbols in the aura. They are usually muddy in colour, coarse in texture and sharp in shape.

'Negative' thought-forms almost always exist within the astral auric body but are sometimes found in the lower mental auric body.

These thought-forms need to be dealt with and processed out of our auric system if we are to get the most out of this physical existence. The job of getting these 'negatives' out is not an easy one. Most often these forms were created long ago in childhood or go back even further to past lives. It takes intensive and consistent delving into our 'old issues' to defeat these thought-forms or belief systems.

We can start by defining the origin of the 'negative' thought-form; who told you you weren't smart enough, pretty enough, thin enough, etc.? Who fed you the negative impressions that helped you to create the personality problems that you struggle with today? These beliefs about yourself were created in the mind of the child you once were. When you look at them with your adult mind you can understand why someone said what he or she did, but the child couldn't see all of the aspects involved. If a child was called a dummy every day by his mother he will grow up with that 'old tape' playing in the back of his mind. Even if he definitely knows he is intelligent (he may even have a Ph.D), he still has insecurities about his intelligence. This will have a dramatic effect on his performance for the rest of his life, unless he begins consciously to deal with these old thought-forms. A thought-form will persist as long as it is fed enough energy to hold its particles together. The more that we dwell on our 'negatives' the stronger the energy of the thought-form. It is in this way that we finally manifest what we most dwell upon. Thoughts are 'things'. Those who spend their lives fearing what will happen next are most likely to create fearful situations to live through. Those who think in hateful ways will bring hateful people to them. Those who believe that they are poor will create only poverty for themselves. Thoughts are powerful, but remember the same power that can destroy can also create.

These 'old tapes' put limitations on an otherwise unlimited potential that we all possess. It is important to examine these old self-limiting messages and begin to create a programme of positive replacements for yourself. Always keep in mind you are creating your own reality at every second by the choices you make with your every thought. Your reality is created out of a string of judgements you have made around what you have experienced over time. This string of judgements begins to form your 'truth'. If what is true for you is destructive or limiting to your unlimited potential you can be certain that it will be visible within your astral auric body as a 'negative' thought-form.

Altering long-term 'negative' behaviour patterns and replacing them with positive ones destroys 'negative' thought-forms. I have used quotation marks around the word 'negative' because I don't believe that 'negative', in the strict sense of the word, exists. A 'negative' is merely a motivating factor. It stimulates, and stimulates, and stimulates you until you take some sort of action to make a change. If you are positive-evolving, the change will be a quantum leap onward and upward on the evolutionary ladder. If you are hanging onto 'negative' or limiting choices the negatives will compound until at last, at the depths of the lowest moments of your life, you see the 'Light' and move at warp speed in the opposite (positive) direction. Some individuals, sadly, do not physically survive this low time in their life and are processed on to a new life at a later time when all of the challenges will be presented to them once again.

Do we have to be blinded, lose our limbs, or be stricken with cancer before we change the way we perceive our world? We have all heard stories of how a major tragedy became the pivotal point in an individual's life. Wouldn't it be better to be aware of the signals that our 'negative' thought-forms are sending to us? By understanding what they are telling us about how we perceive ourselves and our world, we can actively work to replace them with positives, thereby actively participating in our evolvement. Dealing with and transforming 'negative' thought-forms can be a lifetime process or it can take an instant. The choice is always ours.

There is another kind of thought-form that appears in and around the aura.

These are the needle-thin fireworks I see around people with active minds.

These 'positive' thought-forms shoot out away from the head at an incredible speed and disappear as quickly as they appear. There is hardly time to note one before it is gone from sight. They are usually bright white, yellow or pale blue in colour. They can travel in straight lines or quickly arc and disappear. Many times I have seen them explode like a fireworks display, the end of their comet-like heads popping silently out of the level of my vision.

As a student in a psychic development class some years back, I had a teacher who was prolific in the creation of these happy little thought-forms. When his class really got 'cookin'' the room would be filled with sparks. The show would get so intense that I often missed the content of his lectures. I would sit absorbed as he mentally tossed little blue lights at each of us.

Thought-forms are manifestations of the reality we have created for ourselves. 'Positive' or 'negative', they are motivators for our evolvement. They are representatives of our belief systems. It would serve us well to create, transform and otherwise use them to our advantage.

Chakras

Chakras are short, squat, swirling, mini tornadoes of colour strung in an orderly line along the spine from the top of the head to the tailbone. They are energy whirlpools where incoming energy is processed and distributed, and where outgoing is cannoned outward to where it must go.

The student of metaphysics usually concentrates on seven of these centres. There are actually many more chakras besides the major seven, and these are called minor chakras. These minor energy centres can be found in our hands and feet, at each breast, in each knee and elbow, at the hips and shoulders, even at the ankle bones.

There has been much written about chakras in the last two thousand years and for the student who wishes to know more about these centres, I refer you to those volumes. For our purposes here, namely the understanding of ourselves through the study of the aura, I will briefly describe the location and general function of each of the major chakras. By having a general idea of what goes on at any given centre, and locating the disruption or activity in the auric layers near that centre, we can put the two elements together to get a more precise picture of the mental, physical, emotional and spiritual health of a subject.

Some of these centres I see with my physical eyes, although they are usually faint and I have to rely on my Inner Eye as well as explanations from guides and my higher mind to get a clear picture of how they are functioning. It is not important to actually see these centres in analyzing an aura. If one sees a disruption or a

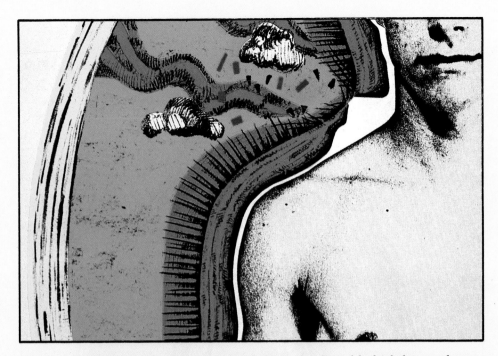

Figure 1 *The Physical Auric Body (white band next to the physical body) bulging at the area of disease or injury. The Etheric Auric Body (represented here in green) is disrupted creating a hole. The Vital Auric Body (represented here in orange) is reduced in width at the area of injury or disease causing the radiant lines to droop giving the appearance of wet fur.*

Figure 2 *Kirlian photograph of the author's fingertips. Two images of the right hand.*

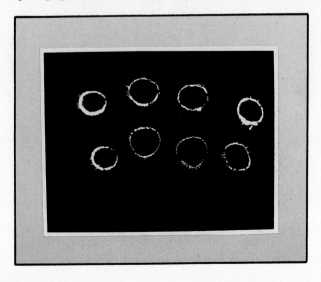

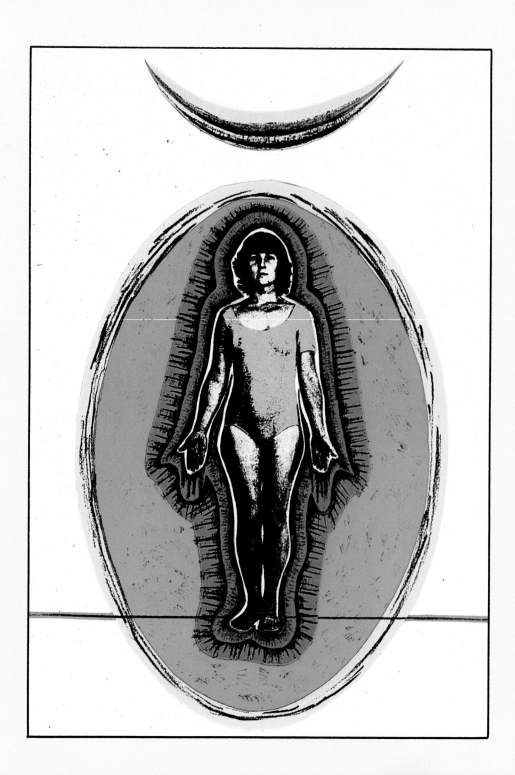

Figure 3 *The auric bodies. (Starting at the outer edge of the physical body.) The Physical Auric Body (represented by a thin white band), the Etheric Auric Body (represented here in green), the Vital Auric Body (represented here in orange), the Astral Auric Body (represented here in blue), the Lower Mental Auric Body (represented here by yellow). The crescent above the head represents the lower edge of the Higher Auric Bodies, the Higher Mental Auric Body (the crescent shape, violet, dark blue and gold) and the Spiritual Auric Body (found in the centre of the ovoid shaped Higher Mental Auric Body).*

Figure 4 *An example of an aura displaying mental illness.*

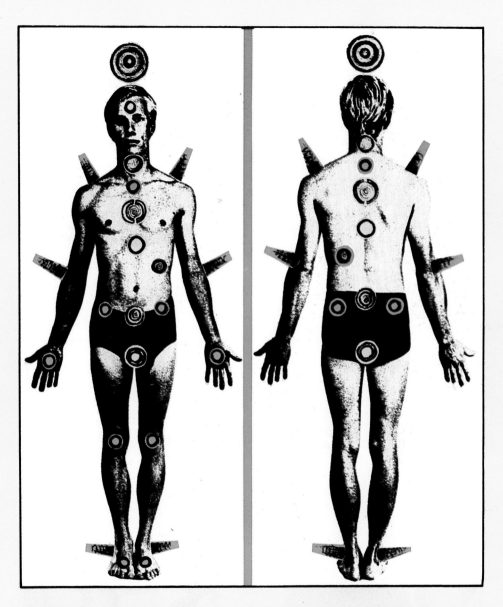

Figure 5 *Other elements present in the aura. Clockwise from lower left spherical-shaped Guide Energy working in the area of the Health Aura (Inner Aura), a meandering (unused) Ray connected to the Sixth Chakra, a Powerful (being used) Ray connected to the Third Chakra, and a small Guide Energy working in the Astral Auric Body.*

Figure 6 *The Chakras. Front and back views of the major (represented in yellow) and minor (represented in blue) chakras.*

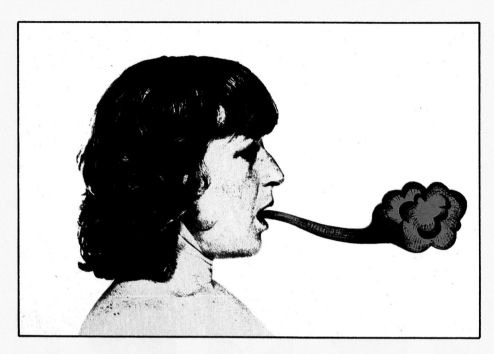

Figure 7 *Colour Breathing. (a) Breathing in the coloured cloud. (b) Exhaling the colour to surround the body.*

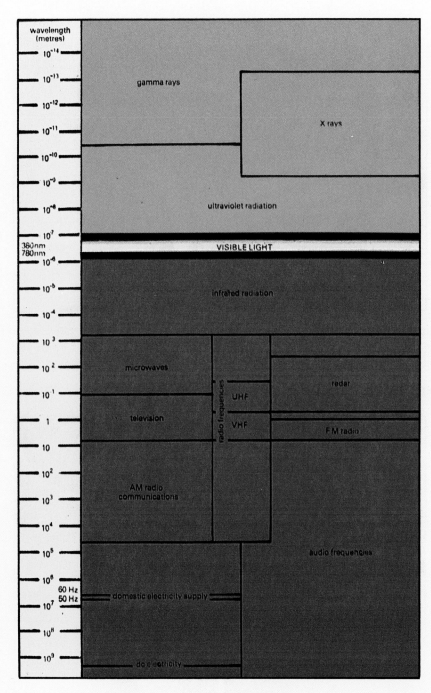

Figure 8 *Chart of the Electromagnetic Wave Spectrum.*

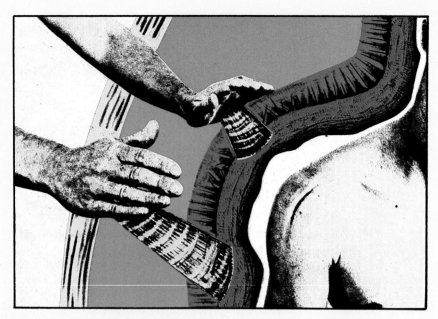

Figure 9 *Healing and sealing the auric layers. In this example both hands are being used to project a lavender energy from the Palm Chakras onto the Etheric Auric Body (represented here in orange). Note the dramatic bulging of the Physical Auric Body caused by the injury on the shoulder.*

Figure 10 *Using a crystal to heal and seal an area of injury.*

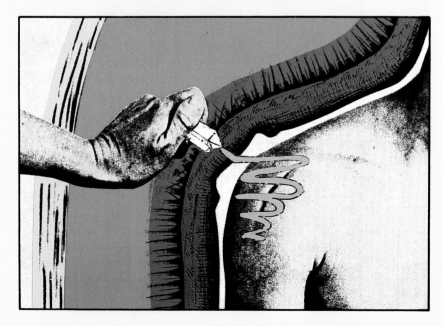

helping ray near the fifth chakra (throat chakra), for example, one only has to know that the fifth chakra is a centre of communication, and depending on the meaning of the colours of the disruption or ray, can assume that the root of the activity is in the area of communication — that is, communication with others or with one's Self.

Traditionally, any listing of chakras starts at the root chakra. Also called the first chakra, it is the centre where our most primitive, autonomic systems are fed their energies — systems that regulate our will to live or the power to operate our immune system, in other words, our basic survival mechanisms.

The first chakra is found at the base of the spine between the sacrum and the coccyx, or tailbone (see Fig. 6).

When disruptions are seen in the auric layers near this chakra the subjects could be suffering (depending on the degrees of disruption) from deep insecurities or immune system malfunctions (such as AIDS) and related diseases. They may display outward symptoms such as greed, theft or a feeling that the world is pushing them around and they have to fight back. They are frightened and they feel that there isn't enough to go round. Disruptions at this centre will create a compulsive personality who is unable to find rest even when surrounded by positive happenings. The basic animal sexual drives are rooted here as well. When disruptions are noted and symptoms of out of control sexual drives are displayed, it is a good bet that the chakra is open too wide, allowing too much base energy in and out. In the case of extreme impotence or frigidity, the flow of energy is cut off at this centre.

On the front of the body, just above the area of the genitals and below the navel, is the second chakra. Its location is often reported to be at the genitals, but I perceive it differently. The area of the spine through which it passes is the lower section of the lumbar vertabrae.

When disruptions are noted near this centre the afflictions are usually of an emotional nature. It is at this chakra that we first process or interpret the emotional world around us. When this centre is seriously afflicted the lower digestive system is affected. The chemical balances in the intestines, colon and stomach are destroyed, ulcers and even various cancers can result. On a temporary, less serious side, we may suffer butterflies in the stomach (something I personally have to deal with before each of my lectures and workshops).

The second chakra is the regulator of our endocrine functions. When a disruption occurs at this chakra the ductless glands such as the pituitary, thyroid, adrenals, Islands of the Langerhans in the pancreas, ovaries and testicles do not secrete their particular potions into the blood-system thus causing imbalance and disease. Outward symptoms may be a general lack of vitality, rapid loss of youthful appearance and a diminished drive to attract others into their life.

Just below the ribcage, at the base of the sternum, is the solar plexus. It is here that the third chakra is found. The energy of this chakra flows through the transition point between the thoracic and lumbar vertabrae of the spine.

The third chakra is the point of personal power and the expression of creativity through the balanced use of that power. Disruptions in the aura at this centre can denote anything from timidity and fear to a powerful drive to express anger and rage. People who are driven to immoral excesses by their ambition have a severely afflicted third chakra, as do those who feel impotent and completely at the mercy of external forces.

The fourth chakra, commonly called the heart chakra, is located in the centre of the chest approximately at the level of the heart muscle, between the ribs on the sternum. The energy of this chakra flows through the mid-point of the thoracic vertabrae of the spine.

This centre is the gatekeeper to the higher chakras. Here the energies from the lower chakras are transformed vibrationally so that they can move on up the system. The transforming power used here is compassion and love. This is the point where we take in and send out our love and we process and distribute the love that we have for our Selves. When this chakra is disrupted lower energies become the driving force, animal lust supersedes human love and compassion. On the other side of the disruption scale, subjects may be so preoccupied with love and compassion that they become absorbed in a 'world of oneness', and find it difficult to participate and survive in this physically demanding world.

We have all experienced a broken heart at one time or another. This has been described as an actual physical feeling of aching emptiness in the chest or like 'dark rain inside an empty cavern in the chest'. Prolonged periods of such distress can lead to heart disease and even death. We can actually die of a broken heart.

Disruptions at the heart chakra can manifest outwardly as a cold personality. Such people are quite devoid of compassion and morality and can be very destructive to society.

Asthma is, in part, a disease associated with fourth chakra disruptions. Its roots go even deeper into the lower chakras, as do many of the diseases associated with this chakra.

The fifth chakra, or throat chakra as it is commonly called, is the centre of communication. Here our abilities to communicate outwardly with others and to communicate inwardly with our Self, are given energy.

The position on the spine where this chakra flows through is the lower cervical vertebrae.

This chakra is associated with the thyroid, the regulator of metabolism. Disruptions in the aura near the fifth chakra can be a sign of metabolic diseases, a neurotic obsession with meaningless ritual, an inability to discipline one's self, excessive vocalizing, or an inability to express one's self.

In the case of those who stutter, I have seen flecks of red lodged in or near the chakra. The red flecks are representative of anger which in this case is not outwardly expressed.

One of the major causes of obesity is the inability to express one's true feelings. When people lock away their self-expression, often covering it up with humour or sarcasm, such 'holding back' slows down the metabolism dramatically, thus affecting how food energies are used. The result is excess weight gain.

Probably the most fascinating of the chakras, and certainly the one which has held the greatest mystique throughout the centuries, is the sixth chakra or the *agna* chakra. This chakra is said to be seated in the centre of the brain and to operate something called the Third Eye. This Third Eye is where your spiritual sight functions, and is often depicted in the centre of the forehead just above the eyebrows.

Modern scientific research suggests that there may be a biological basis for the Third Eye. Current thought about the origin of the eye is that originally the pineal gland, located in the centre of the brain immediately behind the centre of the brow, was a light sensitive organ as well as hormonal regulator. There are lizards today who can still perceive light with this gland by way of a primitive 'eye' located at the top of its head. Certain proteins involved in the processing of light in the retina have been found in the pineal gland including rhodopsin (visual purple), which we have discussed earlier. Melatonin, a hormone that is thought to regulate moods in humans and is known to regulate the seasonal changes in animal behaviour and physiology, was thought to be located only in the pineal gland; however amounts of it have been found in the retina. There is even evidence that in hamsters there are nerve connections between the pineal and the brain suggesting that not only does the pineal receive messages about the day-night cycles from the more specialized eye, but that it passes on messages of its own to the brain. Our eyes may have started as light-sensing, natural-rhythm regulating organs only to become more specialized into the focused vision receivers of today. The pineal gland also became more specialized as we evolved, and gave up its role as a light receiver.

When I look at a person's forehead to analyze the sixth chakra, I always see a symbol there rather than the usual tornado-styled formation. The sixth chakra is the centre for the psychic and mental in the system so it seems appropriate that I would perceive its representation in symbol form. These symbols are usually quite complex and the dissection of one can be a session in and of itself. I have noticed that these symbols can change as I am viewing them. It is sometimes like watching a holographic hieroglyph show. I don't always find meaning in the symbols so I usually suggest that my subject meditate on it for further information.

When disruptions are seen in the auric layers surrounding this chakra the subject could be suffering from mental or psychic distress, sleep disorders, confusion, hallucinations, delusions, eye problems, or hormonal related diseases.

The seventh chakra, or the Thousand Petalled Lotus, sits at the top of the head, at the crown. It is the first centre that is touched by the fresh cosmic energy coming from the Spiritual Body and the last centre from which this energy finally flows when it has been processed correctly and lifted up through the positive-oriented evolutionary processes of the lower chakras. When this chakra is blocked there is no flow either way, life becomes meaningless and stagnant and depression ensues.

The seventh chakra is of a high spiritual order. It is important to the ultimate evolution of our True Self. Any blockages or disruptions must be treated very seriously because without a constant inflowing of vital cosmic energy the organism that is host for our spiritual body will die and our current opportunities to evolve here will be lost.

I have pointed out many negative situations surrounding disruptions in the auric layers in this section but don't forget — negatives are motivators! Dis-eases are opportunities to evolve. All disruptions of the auric fields can be remedied; all it takes is some positive effort and a willingness to grow.

Knowledge of the chakras can be an important diagnostic tool. So too can the understanding of thought-forms, guide energies and the rays give us a better insight into the complexities of the unique entities that we are.

6

Aura Colours and Their Significance

There are an infinite number of shades, tints and hues of colour just as there are infinite degrees of mental, emotional, physical, and spiritual health and other things which represent themselves in the aura as colour. To cover this subject in depth would make this chapter infinitely long; for our purposes here, I will discuss it in basic terms.

In analyzing an aura I work with only a dozen or so colours. While my eyes are sharply attuned to aura colours, I have still not trained them to discern between the various nuances of each basic colour. Each shade has a different shade of meaning. I usually rely on my intuitive side, not my eyes, for these shades of meaning. Quite often a layer of aura, say the vital auric body, will display two, three and sometimes four different colours. Some of these colours are seen to be overlaying the general colour of the auric body and some colours lie in patches here and there throughout the body. In our example of the vital auric body, let's say I have perceived a general, overall colour of green, and scattered here and there I see traces of yellow and orange. The radiant lines characteristics of this body are shorter than they should be but they appear to be straight and bright. First I would translate the green as representing a healing process happening in that area. Because the vital auric body is associated with the personality as well as physical health I could add that this healing is occurring on the level of the personality as well. Since green represents growth, I would add that this is a very growthful period for the personality. Adding the colour yellow, which is an indicator of the intellect's involvement in the process, I would say that the healing and growth taking place has been partially brought about by a conscious effort on the part of the subject. The orange tells me that the trauma preceding this healing and growthful time is still slightly present. Orange is a representation of a balancing process in the works. I interpret from this that the trauma was not so far into the past. I can get more clues as to the nature of the trauma by looking to see what chakras are disrupted, or by examining the astral auric body near the oranges for signs of thought-forms or flecks of anger. In a nutshell that's how it works. You can see then that it is very important to understand what the colours in the aura mean.

I believe it is indispensable for the student observer to keep a notebook listing colours noted in the aura, and the observer's interpretation and subject's opinion regarding that interpretation. In this way, the definitions for the colours you observe will be tuned to your particular perceptions. You can't get it all from a book, you must build up what is true for you through your own experiences. I mention this because there is some evidence that we all perceive the same colours slightly differently. What is orange to me may be a shade of red to you.

It is also necessary to consider the background behind your subject. A bright yellow wall or a bookshelf filled with red books is going to change the way you see the auric colour superimposed over it. I have remedied this by bringing my own dark backdrop whenever I work outside my office. Even the colour of the clothes that a subject is wearing will affect the way that you interpret which colours are in the auric layers. Ideally a subject should be nude, but that is a bit much to ask of the average person. I often suggest that subjects wear simple, dark clothing such as a leotard or unprinted T-shirt. I have had to analyze the auras of people wearing fluorescent orange, Hawaiian-print shirts, bright plaid sportcoats — you name it! In such cases one has to rely heavily on one's guides and intuition for constant verification of what the eyes are seeing.

Colours displayed in the aura are different from the spectrum of colours that we are most familiar with. Auric colours are translucent, give off a sense of being alive, and can often have a texture as if they were made of billions of tiny molecules of shimmering energy. The only way to come truly close to creating what they look like artificially would be with computer graphic animation. One day I hope to be in a position to create such a picture. For now, I am content to portray a person's aura 'primitively' with coloured pencils. There is a correlation between the auric colours and the spectrum colours that are set up by the brain as the aura is being viewed, making interpretations possible even though the colours are not the same.

The Greens

Green is a growth colour. Psychologically it brings to mind spring. We can visualize new grass popping up out of the dark soil, small leaves stretching out from the barren branch-ends as the last days of winter slumber fade and the renewal of life begins.

Growth, renewal, life springing forth from death. This process is a reflection of the natural cycles repeated at all levels of life. It is the way of science and nature, it is the way of the process of reincarnation. Spring greens remind us of the hope of survival through life's winters and suggests that perhaps even physical death is survivable.

For Americans, green may suggest money. We have slang names for money like 'greenbacks', 'long green', 'lettuce' and 'the green stuff'. In fact the early leaders of this country were Masons, a secret and mystical order. They made certain that the dollar bill had Masonic symbols on it that have very deep metaphysical significance, such as the pyramid with the all-seeing eye at the top of it. Perhaps they also knew of the particular qualities of the colour green to draw supply from the Universe. Green stimulates supply, cash, food, love — whatever is needed — and can help generate its manifestation. The use of the colour gold with green is the supreme stimulator of supply from the external world.

One important thing the diseased, unhealthy or injured need is healing. Green, being a healing colour, helps stimulate the regeneration of injured tissue and sets the appropriate vibrational tone needed to generate the natural healing process. In the case of various cancers, however, the use of green, chromotherapeutically speaking, is not recommended since it can actually stimulate more unwanted cancerous cell growth.

I am shocked when I think of the thousands of cancer patients who are, at this very moment, trying to fight the disease as they lie helpless in a hospital room that has been painted an institutional green. It would do hospital administrators well to consider the colours used in the various areas of their institutions. The advice of a colour consultant, who understands effects of the various colours both psychologically and physiologically, could enhance and hasten the effects of medical treatment. In the long run the extra cost would be taken care of by the efficiency and better quality of care provided by the simple consideration of colour.

In the aura, the presence of a clear, bright, grass green is a positive sign, which suggests that 'the storm has passed' and growth and renewal processes are happening.

A grass green mixed with a portion of white light makes a nice pastel green representing a peacefully-evolving process.

A dark, silver green, such as the colour of a pine needle, is soothing to the nerves. I recommend it for colour breathing-exercises to soothe and neutralize the nervous chatter of the mind. It can be useful just before meditating or before an important business meeting. Always keep it in your mental first-aid kit for times of stress.

In Chapter 3 I mentioned a smoke-like stratum of green in the astral auric body. This smoky layer is neutralizing and calming an agitated area of the emotional body with silver green. The negative thought forms lodged there are being neutralized by the energy represented by this green to make them easier to deal with.

'The sleeping prophet', Edgar Cayce, reported seeing a sickly lemon green above the heads of those people who were lying to him or otherwise being deceitful. A peacock green (green with a hint of dark blue) in the aura represents an intuitively growthful process that is present.

We've all heard the expression 'green with envy'. People who are envious or jealous will display an ugly, muddy, dark green in the astral or lower mental auric bodies.

There are many other greens found in the aura, each with its own shade of meaning. I have listed above the greens I most commonly see. In the sections to follow I will use the same procedure. For those who wish to explore the meanings of other shades, hues, or tints of colour, I refer you to the Bibliography (see p. 109) for further reading.

The Blues

Of the 6,000 plus registered official colours, over half are different kinds of greens and blues. We have just covered the first 25 per cent of the officially existing colours, now let us examine the next 25 per cent, the blues.

Before going any further, I think it is important to point out that all colour groups have both negative and positive aspects. There are blues that represent the highest of intuitive abilities and blues that represent the deepest of melancholia. All of the colours in the blue group represent the connection of an informational process to the brain.

Psychologically, dark blues are generally cooling, soothing and calming and are excellent for trauma reduction in an accident or injury. If you are the injured party, visualize a deep royal blue pouring quickly through the entire body, cooling and soothing injured areas. For myself, I have stopped serious pain within my body in as quickly as two minutes. If you are administering aid to an injured person you can send dark blue out from the chakras in your palms. This, of course, is in addition to administering the physical aid which would normally be given. Do not use dark blue with unconscious persons or those who exhibit signs of shock.

Dark blue is an excellent visualization tool for use in cases of insomnia.

Not too many years ago I met a young woman who was having trouble getting up in the morning and getting off to work on time. In trying to work out a solution to this problem we considered the possible motivational factors: perhaps she did not really like her job, or perhaps a part of her was sabotaging her drive to succeed in her career. She explained that she loved her job as news director at a local popular radio station. She was excited about her chosen career and had diligently worked toward this job for many years. It had to be something else. I suggested we take a look at her bedroom to see if I could find a clue there. One look and the problem was evident. The walls were painted a beautiful dark royal blue! What a wonderful environment to go to sleep in, but certainly a difficult one in which to wake up. I suggested she simply go out and buy a nice graphic poster that contained wide areas of orange, red and yellow and hang it up on the wall across from the foot of the bed. When she heard the alarm go off in the morning she was to open her eyes and look at the poster. The red perked up her circulation, the orange stimulated a balanced wakeful activity between mind and body, and the yellow stimulated her thinking processes and got her involved in working out the details of the interesting things happening that day. She rarely ever again had trouble getting out of bed.

The most commonly found blue in the auras I have analyzed is the dark navy blue. When seen in a ray or energy guide it indicates an inpouring of information from the endlessly deep pool of all knowledge.

In the aura's layers it represents varying degrees of intuitiveness. When found in the etheric auric body the intuition is strong and often unconscious. I have seen it in this layer in successful businesspeople, though they often have denied that they were intuitive until I asked them if they frequently made strong important decisions from a gut level. They had to concede that they had. They also often admitted that they 'just knew' the solutions to complex situations when there was no other available information to go on. Talented 'psychics' display this blue in many places within their auras and often have guide energies filled with this colour stationed at the sides of the head near the ears and eyes.

Another common blue is the light sky-blue. I have found this colour represents the student process in the aura. In other words when it is present one can be fairly certain the subject is studying or learning on whatever level it is found. If it is being inpoured by a ray or a guide energy, the subject is being stimulated to learn about something which is important to his or her evolution. This light sky-blue is the optimum colour for the astral auric body. When it is sky blue throughout, the emotional health of the individual is at its most positive.

For the past two years a new colour has shown up in the auric panorama. Either my vision is expanding to see this new addition or all of a sudden it's more common. It is a green/blue mixture called turquoise. I have taken to calling it the 'New Age colour' because it represents positive-oriented obsessive growth. To give you an example of what I mean, let's suppose this colour is in your aura (it usually is found in an energy guide or ray). You are on your way to the office in the morning when you drive past the public library and you decide to drop in for a minute. One hour later you are on the phone telling your boss that you are very ill and will not be in today. You spend the rest of the day reading every book you can get your hands on regarding the subject of dairy farming on the south coast of Tasmania. Insatiably obsessed, your mind is like a sponge and you just can't get enough information. You may not have any idea why you are studying the subject, you just know you must. That's the way the energy that manifests turquoise in the aura affects a person. My example may have been a bit extreme but I assure you the strength behind the example is no exaggeration.

Indigo and Violet

Indigo is a dark blue slightly in transition to a violet. It represents the intuitive and spiritual in combination. Buddhists consider indigo and gold to be the highest colours in terms of vibration. The sixth chakra is vibrationally connected to this colour and it is a good stimulator for it.

When you mix dark blue (unlimited knowledge) with bright red (activity) you get violet. Therefore the colour given off by spiritual activity in the aura is violet which represents activated unlimited knowledge. It is encountered in rays and guide energies in 80 per cent of the auras that I have analyzed. The presence of violet in the rays and guides represents the High nature of the energies being distributed by them. It also tells me that a high degree of protection is present for the activities at hand.

Violet is a powerful colour when used therapeutically. It is very good for use in slowing wild cell growth. Some sources report that it sets up a vibration that makes medication more effective in dealing with disease. Still other sources claim its effectiveness in assisting with bone healing and growth, stomach disorders and fever. Violet is generally considered to destroy germs and heal skin eruptions. Its nextdoor neighbour in the spectrum, ultra-violet, is accepted by established science to perform these functions as well. Violet is an especially good colour for your metaphysical first-aid kit.

Violet is not recommended as a colour to focus on for the novice meditator. Its intense beauty and powerful energy make a return to normal waking consciousness very difficult for the uninitiated. When the novice does 'get back', he is often 'drained' and very tired. For the experienced meditator, a moderate amount of time focusing on violet can be a transforming, highly spiritual experience.

On the spiritually graded colour-scale, violet is number three down from the highest. Number one is white, number two is gold. Just below violet on the scale are the purples. Purples denote the same as the violets but with a lesser degree of power.

An important violet which should be mentioned is lavender. I see this colour very rarely, but when I do see it in the aura I feel very fortunate. It is almost always seen as a part of the spherical complex of a guide energy. When violet is mixed with white (the highest colour) lavender is created. It is the colour of a Master energy. Once in a while a subject comes along who is fortunate enough to have a Master entity working with him or her and it is certainly a previlege to be in the presence of such energy. I have seen the lavender in the energy at the crown chakra once or twice as well, but to see it at all is extremely rare.

The Reds

Stop lights, warning lights, houses of 'ill repute': what do they have in common? Red lights. Red is a colour of activity. It is a lower vibration colour representing the animal element, sense experience, all things physical, and materialistic thinking.

I have seen various reds in the aura but they were seldom of a positive nature. While red is a stimulator of activity and heat and can help to pick up the circulation of those who need it, it is usually an indication of negative elements present in the aura.

Certain reds can indicate anger, selfishness, hate, a quick temper, and murder. I had the opportunity of examining the aura of a man who had killed his father. He showed no outward sign of emotion about the act but his aura told the real story. In the astral auric body were dense patches of a dried blood red, interspersed in it were large red flecks of anger. The murky black of depression and wisps of sadness were everywhere. There were disruptions around most of the chakras. This man's aura was extremely unpleasant to look at, and the vision of it stayed vivid in my mind for many weeks.

Other reds represent passion and lust. It is no coincidence that many bars and nightclubs use red lavishly in their decor. They are trying to stimulate base emotional responses from their customers. Red will cause customers to drink more and will stimulate lustful feelings, all of which will make customers want to come back. To further make the point, try imagining a brightly-lit bar with yellow walls. The atmosphere at such a place might be just what's needed to create a clientele made up of intellectuals who come there to have discussion. Very few alcoholic drinks would be sold but coffee would probably sell well. Sex probably wouldn't be the main topic of discussion in such a place.

There have been a great many experiments with the use of red lights and filters on both plants and animals. These experiments have been conducted by mainline scientists as well as 'fringe' scientists.

One researcher, hearing that madness could be caused by continuous exposure to red light, created a red room. The carpet and walls were painted red, red lights were installed, all of the furniture was painted red. The researcher used himself as a guinea pig and lived in the room for an extended amount of time. His experience was that after a time he really began to enjoy it. He felt very comfortable. I'm sure that it would have driven me into therapy as I have difficulty just sitting in a bar with red lights for any period of time.

Research on plants has shown that red-light exposure has excited growth, creating taller plants than those grown under balanced natural light of equal intensity and conditions. The problem was that the plants grown under red light were spindly and weak with fewer leaves. Red light supplementation for eight hours at night has been used successfully in Europe for the growth augmentaion of commercially-produced flowers and strawberries.

Use of red as a visualization colour in meditation is not recommended as it raises heart rate and blood-pressure. If a person had high blood-pressure to begin with, visualizing red could be very dangerous.

There is some evidence that wearing red clothing can actually incite anger from those near the person wearing the clothes. It can also, depending on the red, induce sexual attraction. People who wear red for prolonged periods of time may find they have very little energy.

A red tent in a snow storm will keep you warmer than a blue one. Psychologically, it is warmer and physiologically, it generates a more rapid circulation, keeping the body warmer.

One pleasure of the red group is the colour pink. The active red is brought into its highest form with the addition of white light. It stands for universal love and is the usual colour of the heart chakra. I have seen flecks of pink in the swirling mass of the throat chakra and in the rays and guide energies. Wherever it appears a loving energy is in force.

Experiments in mood and behaviour control using the colour pink have shown some remarkable results. After painting a prison cell pink, a prisoner suffering fits of violence would be brought in. After only a few minutes researchers noted that the prisoner's behaviour was considerably calmer. After fifteen or twenty minutes the effect of the colour seemed to wear off and the violent behaviour returned. This experiment was repeated time and again with the same results.

Pink is a wonderful colour to include in your metaphysical first-aid kit for use in helping to soothe mental disruptions. When you visualize and send out pink you are sending unconditional love.

Use of the colour apricot (pink with orange) is also helpful in calming an agitated mental state as it has the additional benefit of the balancing orange element in it.

The Oranges

Another activity-generating colour is orange. Orange is a balanced mixture of red (the physical) and yellow (the mental). This colour is probably the one seen most frequently in the hundreds of auras I have analyzed over the years.

The activity represented by the orange is one of constant balancing and harmonizing. It is an element that sorts and files disharmonies into manageable, balanced units that can be dealt with in an ordered manner.

If a subject is recovering from an illness, I will see orange patches or whole layers of it in the health aura. If the illness or distress was of a mental or emotional nature I will see smoky layers of orange moving about in the thought plane aura. Orange signifies the worst has passed and the process of 'repair' has begun.

Usually, orange will give way to a healing and growthful green when the balancing period is over. Orange should always be considered a transition colour in the aura. If, over a reasonable amount of time, orange is still a factor in the same area, it is clear that the subject is stuck, unable to grow. In such a case a counsellor must re-examine the case with his client and dig down once again to the roots of the problem. The subject usually moves out of the orange phase naturally and this is not a problem.

I find it useful to colour-breathe orange when I am tired but still have things to do. It revitalizes mind and body, enabling me to continue for a while longer.

When orange in the aura is muddy looking, it's an indication of laziness. Certain tones of muddiness represent a personality that is repressing something. In cases where the repression is general, I will see a sickly brown/green/orange covering the second and third chakra areas. This often is an indication of severe disruptions in the intestines and colon. Constipation is an outward sign that you are repressing your emotions, sexuality or personal power distribution. If left as it is this condition will eventually worsen, even to the point of turning into a cancer.

Psychologically, orange generates activity and wakefulness. If, for instance, you were having a garage sale and you wanted to generate a lot of activity and sales, would you make your signs in blue? Blue is not the best choice — it may even slow down business. Green would suggest that the buyer is concerned with money it might even suggest that the sellers are money-hungry. A red sign may catch attention for a moment but it will tire out the readers psychologically and they may dismiss the thought of stopping to look. The answer is orange. Orange will stimulate people to reach for their wallets and take action on something they think they want.

Fast-food restaurant chains have spent large sums of money to research the colours needed in the decoration of their stores. They wanted to know which colours would stimulate sales. What they discovered was that orange stimulated the sales and brown stimulated an earthly need to enjoy the sensual pleasures of eating. How often have you gone into one of these places to pick up a quick sandwich and ended up buying much more?

The Yellows

All yellows are representatives of the intellect. Each shade or tint of yellow expresses a type of functioning ability or expression of the intellect, from the craftiness of a mustard yellow to the high thought of a light yellow to the timidity represented by a ruddy yellow.

Several years back, I found myself in total confusion and disorganization trying to run a one-man advertising agency. I attended to sales presentations, wrote copy for newspaper ads, TV and radio commercials, designed graphics and acted in my own commercials. On top of all of that, I had to keep books (which I hated) and stay organized. To help myself to at least be able to concentrate, I painted the wall in front of my desk a bright healthy yellow. It stimulated me to concentrate while I was sitting there, which was a great help. Now, if I had had a yellow car and yellow-tinted sunglasses, and the recording studio and TV stations had been painted yellow, and all of my clients had been kind enough to wear only yellow clothes around me, I would have been able to keep up that balancing act, but as fate would have it, a better life came along.

When yellow is found in combination with, along side of, or overlayed upon any other colour in the aura, it is to be considered as usually conscious mental involvement in the process which is occurring in that area. For instance, a vital auric layer may be a radiant green. As you look more closely you note that some of the fingerlets of energy are yellow. You can then determine that the subject is displaying a strong and growthful vitality and that this has been brought about because of conscious mental effort. The subject has probably been concentrating on a consistent diet and exercise programme that is paying off.

Gold and Silver

When I talk about the colour gold I am not referring to the ochres (which are in the yellow group), I am speaking of the metallic, reflective colour, characteristic of the precious metal gold. This beautiful colour has a blazing quality when it appears in the aura.

I have never seen this gold in an auric layer but it does occur in rays, guide energies and chakras. It supplies protection by its strength and reflective nature, and cleansing and purification by its purity and high vibrational nature.

Gold is an excellent all-purpose colour for every kind of healing. If you have no other colours in your metaphysical first-aid kit you should certainly keep gold there. You simply can't go wrong with it: when in doubt about which colour to use, choose gold. After a physical injury has been cleansed with antiseptic, clean it with gold directed out of your palm chakras. After it is bandaged, bandage it again with gold.

Another important use of the colour gold is in constructing a protective visualization called the protective aura. This exercise could be the most important piece of information you will glean from this book. The process is explained in Chapter 10. It is a method I and many others have used to protect ourselves from all kinds of disruptive external factors.

The cleansing qualities of gold can be used in a meditative visualization to clean the chakras and aura as well as physical systems.

Simply sit comfortably, feet on the floor, arms, and legs uncrossed. Ta[ ]
very deep breaths, each time holding the breath for a few seconds to find any
tension in your mind and body, then releasing that tension with the exhale.

Ground yourself by imagining tubes of lights coming out of your feet and first
chakra. See the tubes sinking into the earth until they reach the centre. Bring up
earths energies through the tubes until you feel them entering your feet and first
chakra. Feel your affinity with the earth, know that you are connected to it and
anchored safely in your chair.

Imagine that in the top of your head there is a door. Open the door and draw
down a blazing gold colour. Bring it down your spine along the chakra system
to the first chakra. See the gold mixing with earth energy. This will ground you
and at the same time will open you up to the higher energy.

Continue drawing down the gold and see it blasting negativity, disharmony, and
illness out of the first chakra. Visualize the negativity and disharmony being thrown
away from you and your aura. See it falling down through the earth to the centre
where it will be purified, cleansed and recycled back to you as healthy energy.

Fill the newly-cleansed, chakra with gold and continue on to the next chakra.
Repeat the cleansing process with all of the chakras.

Next, use the blazing gold to push down through the aura, cleaning out all the
negativity, illness, and disharmony there. I like to use a large disk of gold which
I visualize as just slightly larger than the diameter of my aura. I pass it through
the aura several times, each time making it clearer, sending old thought-forms and
other negatives to the centre of the earth for purification and recycling.

Repeat the process as you visualize cleansing the physical systems, concentrating
on those organs you know are in need of a healing. Again, push out ill health,
disharmony and disruptions, sending them to the centre of the earth for purification
and recycling. Make sure you take your time, cleaning each nerve, each cell and
every atom in your body.

This method of cleaning was taught to me by a very special Master who prefers
to remain anonymous. Since the time that my wife and I studied with him and
learned the method, we have passed it on to hundreds of others throughout this
country. It has always served us well and I hope you will practise it and pass it
on to those that you love.

Silver represents a quickening of the processes of the colours that surround it.
I most often see this colour in guide energies. It shows that energies being supplied
by these guides are going instantly to where they are needed within your system
and there are no delays of processing involved. In this way lessons are learned
quickly and help is received immediately. This fast preparation mechanism supplies
the subject with needed energies for some event of importance that is quickly
coming to the forefront.

As with the gold, silver is a reflective metallic colour. The silver I see looks extremely reflective, almost mirror-like, having qualities of protection like the gold but not nearly as powerful.

The Browns

Brown is not a common colour in most of the auras I analyze. That is, it is rarely seen by itself as a general colour of an auric layer but usually as a muddying effect with another colour. That's not to say that all browns are a negative factor in the aura. There are beautiful, rich, chocolate browns that denote an affinity with the earth. People exhibiting this brown have great abilities in the agricultural sciences. Some rich browns, such as a golden brown, represent industriousness and the ability to organize.

More often than not, however, browns represent a negative influence in the aura. They show an overly materialistic, selfish personality who has regard only for what he can get and keep for himself.

Grey

Another colour that usually represents negative aspects in the aura is grey. When I perceive grey in an aura I also physically 'feel' it as it gives off a suffocating energy. Grey stands for a narrowly-focused mind which is tightly closed and locked. Those displaying this colour (usually in the lower mental and/or astral auric bodies) are extremely conventional and display a total lack of imagination. Outwardly they are cold and hard; when severely afflicted they are friendless.

Grey is one of the colours representing depression. In this case, the depression is intensely self-generating. Grey is most often accompanied by red flecks of anger and black clouds of depression in the emotional body.

This colour is very difficult to look at for long. Most of the grey I have seen in an aura has been outside my counselling work. There are very few individuals who display this colour who would be interested in having their aura analyzed or be even remotely interested in metaphysics.

I once worked for a man whose aura was so cluttered with ugly thought-forms, grey, negative browns, black, and slashes of various reds, that he was painful to look at. Each successive day that I worked there it became more and more difficult to see him. I tried to avoid him whenever I could but that was nearly impossible.

It finally got so bad, I would wince everytime he came into my vision. Naturally, he began to take my wincing personally and started sending his anger in my direction. It wasn't long before I was fired. So for those readers who think the ability to see auras is always a wonderful thing, remember this story. I always try to control what I have to see, but as I have said earlier, some auras just stand out like sore thumbs.

Black and White

I wore a black shirt today, but it wasn't really black. No shirt, blouse, dress, or sock is black. Never in the history of mankind have any black clothes ever been made. I am, of course, speaking only in the strictest sense of the word, for black is not a colour at all. True black is the absence of light. The black shirt I wore today is actually a very dark brown.

It is the same with white. A true white has never been made. It exists beyond normal vision. All we ever see of it are its components in the visible spectrum.

It is said that at death one is drawn out of one's body and sent through a dark tunnel at an incredible speed. At the end of the tunnel is a blinding white light; this is true white.

Whereas black is the absence of light and colour, white is all colours and the absolute presence of light.

When I refer to black in the aura, such as the black clouds of depression, what I am actually describing is an area where the light has been eliminated, sort of a 'black hole' in the aura. Like the black holes of space, no light can exist in the presence of this black. Wouldn't it be interesting if the astronomers discovered that black holes were actually enormous pockets of emotional depression in the aura of the universe?

The use of white light in visualizations and meditations is not recommended for the novice as the beauty of white light attracts all beings at every level of existence and some of these beings or energies are not positive and are difficult to deal with. However, white light is very protective and while it is being used nothing can enter your aura. After you stop there is a chance that these discarnate energy beings may still be hanging around. To be safe in the use of white I always suggest using white's guardian colour, gold, in combination with it. I will discuss this further when we cover the protective aura.

When white or black combine with aura colours they alter the colour positively (white) or negatively (black). Remember that a clear, bright aura is a healthy one and a muddy, dark aura is an unhealthy one.

Colour Breathing

I have talked a great deal about using the colours discussed above to heal and correct energy levels and have recommended using a technique called colour breathing. Colour breathing is a visualization technique that collects and directs the particular vibrational qualities of the colour or colours being used to the whole body. It will affect every cell of the body, and will concentrate especially on those areas of disharmony. This technique should be an indispensable part of your metaphysical first-aid kit.

Colour breathing is a simple technique for those who have no trouble visualizing. For those who do have difficulty with visualizations, especially where colours are concerned, I suggest trying an eyes-open tactic, concentrating on a swatch of the colour that you are trying to use.

Any visualization or meditation should begin with a grounding technique such as the one we talked about in the section on the colour gold and its use to clean the chakras (see p. 62).

After grounding yourself, visualize or look at the colour you have decided to use. For the sake of this example, let's use the colour orange. Imagine a small cloud of orange is gathering approximately 10 ins (25cms) from the end of your chin. Take a deep breath, slowly drawing in some of this orange cloud. As you exhale, imagine you are blowing out colourless air. The orange cloud in front of you contains an infinite amount of the colour, you can never run out of it. Take another long inhalation, drawing it deeper into your lungs. As you exhale this time, see orange coming out of your lungs and gathering as a cloud around your body (see Figs. 7a and 7b). Continue to draw in greater and greater amounts of orange. As you exhale see the orange coming out of every pore of the skin, pushing out negativity and disharmonious energies. Imagine the orange gathering around your body, energizing and coating the physical body. The orange is soaking into every molecule as you draw it in. Orange will give you a 'second wind' if you are tired. It will energize and harmonize all of your systems whether they are physical or aurical. Other colours have different effects. Blue will have a calming effect, yellow will stimulate the intellect and so on.

The importance of colour in our daily lives, both physiologically and psychologically, is just beginning to be understood and appreciated by the scientific community. In the future colour will take its rightful place in the bag of important tools used by the medical/psychological community.

7

The Historical Aura

This book would not be complete without a short discussion about those individuals who have been concerned with human electrical fields in times past. Most of the books on this subject were written from the research and philosophical thought of men from the turn of this century. Their thoughts and experiments have been rehashed and reprinted in pieces and collections with contemporary covers so often it's difficult to find the newer books on the subject. Since these books are so readily available I won't spend time discussing the experiments and philosophies in detail. Instead, I will present each of those individuals that I feel contributed something of interest to the bank of knowledge on auras. Further study of these pioneers and their contributions will be left up to the reader.

The subject of auras has been with us for many centuries. From ancient Egypt and China to England in the nineteenth century, the human aura has stimulated thought and experiment from many levels of society.

Colour and the aura go hand in hand. No history of the aura would be complete without a bit of information on the history of the use of colour in healing. Colour has been an important tool in the history of healing. The ancient Persians used a form of colour therapy based on the emanations of light from the patient. The ancient Egyptians used coloured stones and amulets as well as elaborate colour-healing temples. Pythagoras, the Greek philosopher of the sixth century BC, used musical vibrations, colour and poetry to cure disease. Colour interacting with the human electrical field has played an important role in the health and welfare of mankind down through the ages. The discoveries of physical science have from time to time overshadowed the more mystical treatment of disease but chromotherapy (the use of colour in the treatment of disease) has always returned as a viable alternative to coarser treatments such as surgery and the intrusion into our systems of strong chemicals.

Ancient Art and the Aura

A quick perusal of any art history book will show the reader that auras are a part of the religious cultures of India and China. In both cultures the deities are shown encased in layers of flames or radiance. Later on, as the Christian religion became prevalent in Western culture, auras were painted around angels, Jesus and the Holy Family. You will also note in these paintings, the presence of a halo. Due to the fact both that the aura's energy is very strong around the area of the head, and that Jesus of Nazareth was an advanced being, this brightening of the aura could have been witnessed by many individuals. Another possibility is that what was being represented as a halo was actually the energy at the crown chakra. If you will remember, the energy represents itself in a collection of concentric spheres near the top of the head. I have seen several people in my investigations who have had very large spheres of light there, looking similar to the halos represented in Christian art.

Avicenna

During the Dark Ages in Europe much of the development of healing practices became dormant. An Arabian by the name of Avicenna (AD 980-1037), led the evolvement of medical history through that period from his part of the world. His *Canon of Medicine* became the most important reference book of the period. In it he proposed that colour was an important curative as well as a guide in diagnosing disease. In diagnosing, Avicenna did not use the auric colours, rather he used colour of skin, eyes, hair and faecal matter. Modern medical personnel use the outward appearance of the patient, such as redness around eyes, yellow skin tone, etc., as a part of their diagnostic process. Avicenna was one of the first to publish the fact that the colour red increases circulation.

Paracelsus

Theophrastus Bombastus von Hohenheim, an alchemist who was born the year after Columbus sailed off to discover the New World, was considered to be a pivotal influence in the evolution of science by the renowned scientist/science historian, Jacob Bronowski. Better known as Paracelsus, von Hohenheim is, to this day, revered by many as the greatest healer of all times.

Paracelsus claimed that a vital force could be found within the human form and that it radiated outward as well, in the form of a sphere of light. He also believed that this envelope of light could be used to heal the physical body.

The Swiss-German physician lived at a time when medicine was divided into two camps, the alchemists and the clinicians. The clinicians were generally educated men who had studied the physical body systems. They sat above their patients during surgery and directed labourers in the actual cutting and repair or removal of diseased tissue. Paracelsus, residing in the other camp, called these physicians 'butchers'. He was so outspoken in fact that he once burned the medical books written by Galen and Avicenna at the beginning of his lecture series in Basel. He complained that so-called modern medicine had left the ways of nature and created an artificial system of treatment and was concerned that the doctors were only out to pick the pockets of the sick. Paracelsus was determined to lead medicine back into the realms of the spiritual.

He created many natural cures for a variety of diseases using the vibrations of music and colour as well as charms, herbs and divine elixirs. Paracelsus was hailed as a great healer in his time for his successes with a multitude of diseases from the common cold to the plague, epilepsy, headache, and insomnia.

He postulated that colours in the vital envelope and those to be used in the healing process could be divided into two groups, those tinged with white representing health and goodness, and those tinged with black representing disharmony, illness and evil.

Mesmer

Franz Anton Mesmer, an eccentric Viennese doctor (1734-1815), believed that everything in the universe was connected by a life-sustaining fluid in which all were immersed. He was also convinced that this fluid energy could be transferred to others to stimulate the healing process.

Because of his sometimes outlandish methods, theories and dress during healing sessions, many prominent scientists of the time labelled him a quack. Among them was the famous American inventor/philosopher/statesman, Benjamin Franklin. Franklin organized a commission of his peers to discredit Mesmer in 1784.

Despite Mesmer's style, his work with animal magnetism carried on, evolving into the practice of modern hypnotism. In some circles hypnotism still carries a stigma from those early days.

Early Plant Research

In 1783, a Frenchman by the name of Tessier began experiments with plants using colour. Thus began over two hundred years of colour research with plants. In relatively recent times (1923) biologist Alexander Gurwitsch discovered extremely low-level energy being given off the plants he was studying. He labelled it 'mitogenetic energy'. His experiments, which were later replicated by other scientists, showed plants have what metaphysicians would call an aura.

Pancoast

Interest in chromotherapy and the aura faded for many years as 'modern' physical science forged ahead with the use of chemistry and the new technology of the industrial age. People were in love with machinery and microbes. Three-quarters of the way through the nineteenth century a man named S. Pancoast published a book called *Blue and Red Light* (1877) in which he described the various healing qualities of blue and red lights.

This rather egocentric man boasted cures for a vast array of disease using natural sunlight through panels of coloured glass. The public became enthralled with his techniques and chromotherapy once again caught their interest.

The revival of colour therapy spread quickly until it was the most important form of healing used in many parts of the Western world. Chromotherapists of all degrees of talent and knowledge cropped up everywhere. Once again there were two camps in the healing world, and the AMA (the American Medical Association) didn't like it.

Babbitt

At nearly the same time as Pancoast's book came out, another book hit the marketplace. *The Principles of Light and Color* (1878), by a man named Edwin D. Babbitt, MD, became the chromotherapist's bible. Babbitt was a 'Renaissance man', a writer/philosopher, physician and artist. His works easily won the hearts and minds of the people and he was soon heralded as the 'miracle man of healing'. Incorporating his theories, many Victorian homeowners installed coloured glass in their windows, many thousands of which are still in place to this day. The custom of coloured-glass windows has recently found a new popularity in our times, though for aesthetic, rather than health reasons.

Babbitt developed several healing 'devices'. One such tool was the 'chromo lens'. Chromo lenses were actually bottles made of various colours of glass constructed so they could be hung in front of a light source. Water was placed in the 42 oz (1 litre) bottles and 'charged-up' in the light. After a period of time the patient would ingest the treated water. Another device called a 'chromo disk' narrowed the light being used to treat the patient down to a focused beam to work specific areas. Babbitt also use a cabinet which he called the 'thermolume' which used natural sunlight. He later added artificial light, using an electric arc lamp. The AMA aggressively attacked Babbitt's findings, denying that the visible spectrum had any curative powers, and the age old battle raged on.

Leadbeater/Besant

Coming from a more philosophical viewpoint, Charles W. Leadbeater, a Theosophist, approached the subject of the aura in several works. Perhaps the most famous is a book called *Man Visible and Invisible* (1920). My favourite of his works is one which he did with Theosophist President and author of many lectures and books of philosophy, Annie Besant. The book, entitled simply *Thought-Forms*, has several pages of colour plates illustrating thought-forms which look very much like the ones I have observed over the years.

Kilner

There was a doctor who, affiliated with London's St Thomas' Hospital at the turn of the century, set out to examine the phenomenon known as the human electrical field. Being a medical person with an ever-watching scientific peer group, this doctor, Walter J. Kilner, began a series of experiments designed to research the aura, eliminating the mystical elements.

Kilner developed a screen through which he and his assistants could view the basic shape and structure of the aura in 1908. The screen was constructed of two panes of glass in a frame. Between the glass was a solution of alcohol and a coal-tar solution of dicyanin, which he called 'spectauranine'. He used several of these screens with various dilutions of alcohol to look at the different levels of the aura.

The large volume of metaphysical literature on the aura was avoided by Dr Kilner until he had studied some 60 patients and documented his observations. He did not want to prejudice his interpretation of what he was seeing in any way.

He found that over a period of time his ability to see the aura increased with constant exposure to the screens but it also had a negative effect on his eyes and he found that he had to discontinue use of the screens for several days to get normal vision back. He also discovered during this period without the use of the screens that he had developed the ability to see the 'human atmosphere' without them.

Kilner published his detailed and careful research in his book 'The Human Atmosphere' (1911). The book's release caused quite a stir among his more conservative colleagues and Kilner found himself caught up in the kind of trouble he had worked so hard to avoid.

Bagnall

Oscar Bagnall, a Cambridge biologist fascinated with Dr Kilner's research, set out to duplicate his experiments. Bagnall used the Kilner screens as well as screens of his own design in different colours. His findings were published in his book

The Origin and Properties of the Human Aura (1937).

Bagnall was unable to replicate all of Kilner's research, though he did not doubt his findings. He determined that Kilner had to be somewhat clairoyant, a talent Bagnall did not feel he himself had.

The Cambridge biologist postulated that all living things have an aura, and that with the cessation of life, the aura also ceases to exist. He was the first to suggest that auric light was perceived with the rods in the receptor field of the eye and was not seen by focused, but rather, peripheral vision.

Dinshah

Inspired by the works of Babbitt, an Indian-American inventor by the name of Dinshah Ghadiali set out to construct colour projection devices and theories with a more scientific base to help to heal mankind safely and gently. Dinshah toured the United States lecturing and demonstrating his new colour therapy methods and devices. Again, the AMA was outraged and set out to destroy his growing practice. For forty years Dinshah fought legal battles in the courts. The US government tried to take his citizenship away but lost the battle. He was convicted on the Mann Act (transportation of a minor female across state lines) when he took his secretary on his lecture tour. Later President Roosevelt granted him a full pardon on the trumped-up charges. Dinshah, undaunted, continued his healing work and established his Spectro-Chrome Institute on 23 acres in Malaga, New Jersey. From this centre he taught his principles of colour therapy and conducted further research. Then, suddenly, his laboratories caught fire. Irreplaceable records and research were lost. Not long after that the FDA (Food and Drug Administration) took him to court again. With no records to back up his claims he lost the suit. The US Post Office refused to deliver his devices through the mails. All over America federal agents raided homes that had Dinshah's healing devices, confiscating and destroying them. Finally, in 1947, the FDA filed a criminal suit against Dinshah. The trial lasted for a month and a half. Dinshah presented hundreds of exhibits and nearly 200 witnesses for his case. He lost. He was fined $20,000 and sentenced to five years probation. All of his books and instruments were destroyed by the federal government.

Dinshah picked up the pieces after his probation period had ended and carried on promoting his theories until his death in 1966.

Recent Times and Beyond

As time goes on and technology becomes more sophisticated, we find the world of science and the world of metaphysics share more and more common ground.

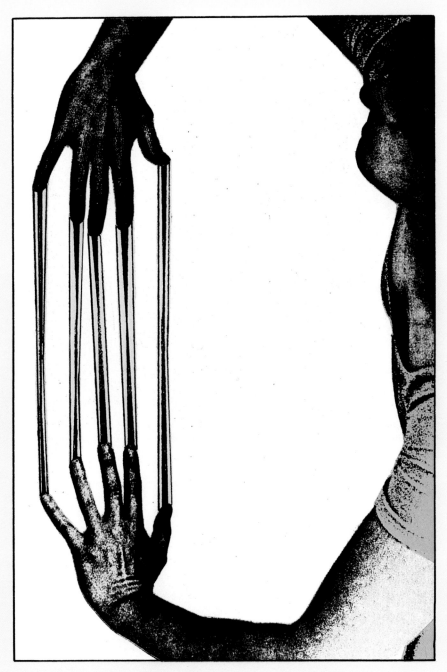

Figure 11 *Classic aura viewing exercise. (a) Noting the way that the energies exiting the fingertips of one hand connect with the energies of the other hand.*

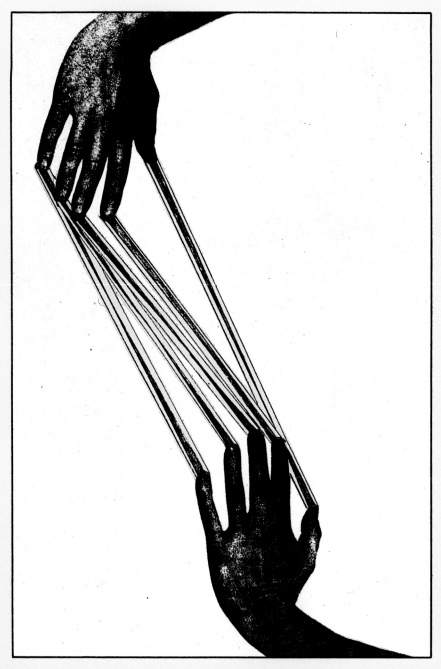

Figure 11 *Classic aura viewing exercise. (b) Moving the hands, the lines remain connected.*

Figure 12 *Author's example of an Aura Portrait.*

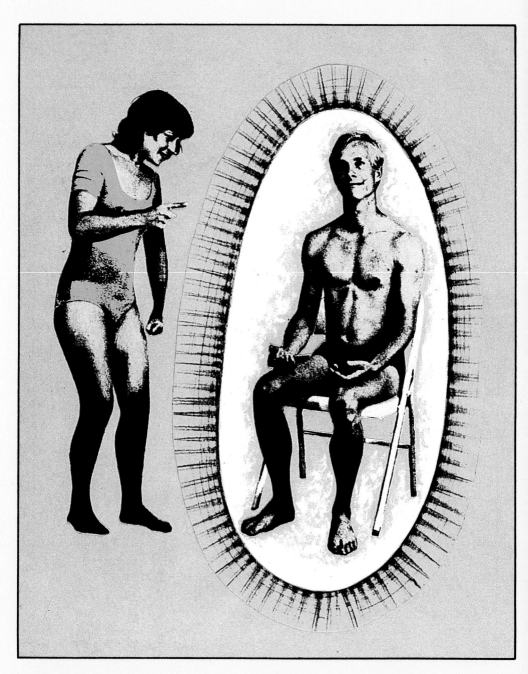

Figure 13 *Using the Protective Aura as an insulation against an angry person.*

As modern researchers in physics attempt to explain and revise the laws of the physical universe, to their surprise they step into a realm once only explored by the mystic. Questions about our physical universe are becoming more complex and esoteric and so are the answers. Like it or not, both camps will one day find themselves united.

Albert Einstein explained to us that there is no such thing as matter, that matter was an illusion created by the vibrational speed of various forms of energy. Things we perceive with our slowly vibrating senses are energies vibrating at the same slow rate. All things that vibrate within what we call the physical range appear to us to be solid matter. Science has shown that when any object is reduced down to its 'smallest' particle, it is made up of millions of sparks of energy. Our sun and the stars, relatively speaking, are sparks of energy.

The implication of this revelation is that if there is a whole world vibrating at one particular frequency, might there not then be an infinite number of other worlds vibrating (here and now) in our universe as well?

Methods of travelling great expanses of space by UFOs, apparitions, apports and many other things now classified as occult, may have to be reclassified by the scientific community as the bank of scientific knowledge mounts up.

Astronomer Gustaf Stromberg suggested that form in the physical is manifested by wave forms originating in the non-physical universe (a different speed of vibration of energy) and returns to that universe when physical life (this vibration of energy) ends.

The research of Harold S. Burr and F.S.C. Northrop of Yale University no doubt had an effect on Stromberg's theories. Northrop and Burr's experiments using ultra-sensitive electro-magnetic wave measuring devices on laboratory animals showed auras diminish and totally disappear at the moment of death, while cells continue to live for a period of time. If where there is life there is an aura, then when there is no longer life where is the aura? Is anything lost in our universe or is it simply changed? Why is there a measurable weight loss at the instant of death? Science is just inches away from proving existence after death.

Edgar Cayce's approach to the aura, though more metaphysical than scientific, showed important correlations between certain auric colours and various traits of health and personality. His contribution to the bank of knowledge of the aura was, sadly, a small one as he died shortly after writing his only pamphlet on the subject (*Auras*, 1945).

Photo-biologist John Ott further added to our knowledge of the effects of various forms of light on living organisms through his research found in his book *Health and Light* (1973). His research over the past fifty years has yielded important information that society is only just beginning to put to practical use.

Aura research continues. With technological advances such as better, faster computers, the pooling of international research along with the development of more and more sensitive EM wave-measuring devices, the possibilities for understanding the aura grows. The only limiting factors are a lack of adequate funding of EM wave-research projects and a traditionally conservative, violently prejudiced, established scientific community.

Consider the case of Dr John Zimmerman, assistant professor of psychiatry at the University of Colorado School of Medicine.

I first met Dr Zimmerman at a symposium in Denver in 1985. I was delivering my lecture on 'The Aura and Health'. A man in the centre of the first row kept coming up with the most intelligent and profound questions for me throughout the lecture. The questions were certainly not the standard ones I'm usually asked; they were specific, often complex, and I must admit I wasn't able to answer some of them.

After my lecture, the man approached me and said that much of what I had been talking about in my lecture concerning the nature and structure of the aura was very similar to his findings. He suggested I attend his lecture on the following day.

The next day I sat in on his lecture. He introduced himself as Dr John Zimmerman, a professor at the University of Colorado and Co-Director of the Regional Sleep Disorder Centre at the Medical School there.

He described his basement laboratory at the school and projected slides of a special 2 ins (5cms) thick aluminium isolation booth which is lined with eggshell foam rubber. He also described a very sensitive EM wave-measuring device which he called a SQUID (Superconducting Quantum Interference Device). With the SQUID he is able to measure a very small portion of the aura's waves. By moving the device to several adjacent areas, a pattern can be set up; however the pattern will not reflect what is happening at a given moment but rather several moments. With a multiple array of SQUIDs, Zimmerman would be able to get a picture of a large area in real time. To illustrate this concept, Dr Zimmerman holds up a drinking straw and peers through it at an object to show what one SQUID will do. Then he holds up a bundle of drinking straws and looks through them at the object, thus demonstrating how much more several SQUIDs can perceive.

Unfortunately due to the lack of funding for projects that appear to be on the fringe of established science, Dr Zimmerman has thus far only been able to construct one SQUID.

The medical usage of Zimmerman's device, which he calls the BMI (Bio-Magnetic Imager), could prove invaluable one day. It would replace the scanners currently in use such as the PET (Positron Emission Testing) scanner and the NMR (Nuclear Magnetic Resonance) imager. Zimmerman demonstrated that the BMI was not invasive upon the physical body and did not use radioactive isotopes in its scanning. Not only is it safe to use in diagnosis but it presents data more accurately by presenting complete visual resolution in both time and space of the brain's activity. 'If that weren't enough,' says Zimmerman, 'the BMI is dramatically less costly than the current methods of scanning.'

As Dr Zimmerman's lecture continued I realized that he really was measuring the human aura. He described the area closest to the body as being much more dense than areas further out from the body. Also he showed an in/out flow at the top of the head at the crown chakra. He has measured exiting energy in the palm of the hands that appears to be in a swirling pattern, a good description of the palm chakras as I see them. While his mapping of the aura is still in its infancy, it most often correlates with my observations.

As the lecture went on I heard terms like 'magneto-encephalo-graphy' (MEG), 'magnetic flux lines', and 'magneto miograms'. He talked about the dramatic success he has had with measuring the healing process while a hands-on (therapeutic touch) healer sent energy to a series of patients in the booth.

Researchers in other labs across the US such as New York University's Neuromagnetism Laboratory have shown similar results. They forge on in their quest to understand and improve diagnostic and healing procedures, but even as in the days of Paracelcus, new thought and procedure is not accepted easily or without risk.

Funding and archaic attitudes have become difficult hurdles for John Zimmerman. After an article showing the results of his experimentation with healers was published, Zimmerman was denied the use of his laboratory by the powers-that-be at the University.

His SQUID and other equipment now unavailable to him, he hit the lecture circuit speaking in such diverse places as China and Great Britain where he has found open ears and minds interested in his research. Articles about his research have appeared in such prestigious trade papers as *Brain and Mind Bulletin*. Some financial interest has been generated but not enough. Zimmerman has recently found a new home for his laboratory in the Denver area at the School of Nursing of the University of Colorado, but as of writing this book, a new booth and SQUID have yet to be created.

In time, with appropriate funding and a shifting of attitude in the scientific world, this important researcher, like so many before him, will once again contribute to our scientific and metaphysical knowledge. Dr John Zimmerman and those to follow will one day open the doors for a new medicine, the truly holistic, non-invasive medicine of the New Age.

8

The Aura and Healing

As we have seen in the last chapter, the relationship between the aura and the healing process has been a primary focus for metaphysicians throughout history.

Illness is what happens to our physical systems when we are in disharmony. Wellness is harmony. Harmony can be defined as the pleasing interaction, or appropriate combination, of the elements as a whole. As was mentioned in an earlier chapter, disharmonious ('negative') energy affects the frequency and amptitude of normally-functioning, healthy cells, altering the auric emanations.

Disharmony can be caused by many events and attitudes: lack of self-worth, the death of a close relative or friend, fear, guilt, depression — the list goes on and on. Even 'accidents' are drawn into our experience by our subconscious needs. While this statement may seem a bit outrageous to some, we must remember that all beings are linked on some level or levels of consciousness, and in close proximity, by the vital auric body. Two people, for whatever reasons of evolvement or self-testing, who need to have an automobile accident, will find each other on the highway. We always attract those people and situations that we most need to further our education in this realm. The power behind the situation drawn to us usually varies, depending on the level of conscious awareness and participation in our evolvement process. The more awake we are to the fact that all of our earthly experience is a growthful learning experience, the more easily processed they are. This does not mean the actual events are necessarily easier, often they are not. What it does mean is that because we are consciously participating in our evolving process we are going with our life's natural flow, and less disharmony is created.

Most of the trouble we get into in our lives comes from repeating our 'mistakes'. Repetition of lessons that have not been learned the first time create a compounding of the power behind them the next time around. Avoidance of important issues in our lives causes a build-up of disharmonious energy in our physical cells. The vibration rate of the cells becomes out of harmony with surrounding cells. Defence mechanisms of the body begin their attack on the disharmonious cells. Chemical activity in the area changes. Eventually a subtle symptom registers in the conscious mind. Usually symptoms are ignored until the individual is actually incapacitated. Unable to function, we finally consult a doctor. By this time the disruption has become very powerful and the doctor's task is more difficult than if we had heeded the early symptoms.

When viewing the aura, we can see these disruptions before they get to the physical symptom stage. The sooner we get an accurate diagnosis and treatment, the better.

Modern medicine can, in most cases, provide diagnosis only after the patient reports physical symptoms. The course of action then is to treat merely the physical body, eliminate the symptoms, thereby hopefully eliminating the illness. The root causes are traditionally ignored.

What do I mean by 'root causes'? Consider this example. A young woman, DG, age twenty-nine, went to her doctor complaining of severe stomach pains which she described as 'a feeling that someone had stuffed wet rags' in her belly. The doctor examined her, asked a few questions, then ordered an X-ray examination. DG reported to the hospital X-ray lab and was given a barium meal to drink. The drink filled her stomach with light radioactivity and the pictures were taken. Later, the doctor determined from the X-ray pictures that DG had two small holes in the lining of the duodenal section of her small intestine. He ordered medication and a severe diet change to which DG complied. In a few months the condition had greatly improved so the medication and diet were eliminated. Six months later DG collapsed and was taken to the hospital; the ulcers had returned with a vengeance.

If a doctor trained to view auric layers had examined DG he would have compiled, in addition to the physical information, more data on which to base his treatment. The disruption in the area of the stomach would have shown the root causes stemmed from anger and depression noted between the areas of the second chakra (emotion processing) and the third chakra (personal power distribution). The chakras were impeded and unable to function properly. He might have determined from this that DG was experiencing some major stresses where her personal power was concerned. He could have determined that she was probably feeling powerless in some situation that had great importance for her. His next course of action would have been to question her regarding these matters, directing his search in the areas of self-image, feelings of inadequacy and self-consciousness, relating to others, etc., to define more exactly what was generating the disharmonic vibrations. Together, DG and her aura/physician would have narrowed down the probable external stimuli, in this case feelings of inadequacy and unworthiness in her job situation. DG was intimidated by her supervisors, who she said 'make me feel stupid'. Further enquiry showed that as a little girl she was always told by her father that she was stupid and could never do anything right. Her young mind imprinted this information in the form of a belief system. It joined the vast number of impressions her brain was storing up regarding what she believed she was. This particular tape played back every time she was face to face with an authority figure such as a supervisor. Emotionally, each encounter took its toll until one day her physical body began to ache. The emotional pain got so bad that it began to eat away at her body. The physical pain was a signal for help to be sought. As I have said earlier, 'negative' events (such as this one) are simply our way of getting our own attention regarding matters that we are not dealing with consciously. Eventually all of our disharmonies are brought to our attention so we can deal with them and move ahead.

DG's poor self-image and belief that she was inadequate caused her to make a lot of mistakes on the job. Each mistake brought to her attention by a supervisor became one more piece of evidence that what she believed about herself was correct. The actual truth is that DG is very intelligent and scored highly in school. Her company was extremely happy to hire her and had very great expectations of her. DG always tried hard to please her father, who could never be pleased. Confronted by authority in the workplace, the pattern continued. With each upsetting episode, the vibrations which were maintaining the equilibrium of her cells became disrupted and vibrated out of sequence with the surrounding cells. In an attempt at harmony, nearby cells at first fight the disruptive vibrations. Eventually the vitality, the 'food' of the cell-forming energy, runs down. The weakened cells begin to vibrate at a disharmonious rate in an attempt to seek harmony. Thus the disharmony is able to expand and grow, compounding to create eventually, in this case, the death of many of the cells in the duodenum, thereby creating ulcers.

I have never advocated the elimination of doctors. Modern medical science is truly miraculous. I would simply like to see the addition of aura-viewing techniques to the varied skills of the physician. Such a doctor would, in addition to medicine and dietary considerations, help the patient to explore the psycho-emotional and spiritual aspects at the root of what is causing the physical distress. Such treatment would include the use of affirmations to help over-ride old belief systems and replace them with new, positive beliefs. Creative visualizations such as colour-breathing or focusing on a new self-image might be prescribed. Therapeutic touch methods or hands-on healing could be employed to help adjust the vibrational disharmony. All of these methods are non-invasive and help patients to be more focused and involved in their own healing process. Most doctors will admit that they merely assist in the healing process; it is the patient who does the healing. When patients eliminate the root problem, not only are they healed, but they have also learned something, they have grown. Each obstacle that is eliminated allows a patient, such as DG, to take another step closer to realizing her full potential so she can participate 100 per cent in the joys of this lifetime.

One day in the future all patients will check into a clinic for a day to experience a battery of physicians and healers of all disciplines who will use their talents to eliminate holistically once and for all the root causes of disease and trauma of all kinds.

Today, all over this country, new holistic clinics are being set up. The medical personnel at these clinics are pledged to examine and treat the whole person. As we become a more enlightened society these clinics will become the norm and we will grow healthier for it.

It is the responsibility of the consumer to be aware of the possibilities for medical treatment in the community. Care should be taken to choose a doctor or clinic that is aligned with the philosophies of the holistic approach. As consumers we have the power to create the kind of medical care we want by simply not supporting those with limited belief systems.

Good health is not only a harmonious functioning of the physical body, it is harmony of, and between, the spiritual, mental, and emotional bodies as well!

Visible Light and the Healing Process

Visible light is an important medicine for healing on the auric level. Visible light effects changes in the vibrational rate of auric emanations. In so doing, it affects the subtle bodies as well as the physical body. To discuss healing in the aura we must also discuss the physical effects of coloured light of the visible spectrum.

We have learned that all matter is energy in vibration. Various energies vibrate at different frequencies — rocks vibrate at a different frequency than radio signals, a gamma ray and the colour blue vibrate at different frequencies.

The visible spectrum, red through violet, represents a very small section on the chart of known EM waves (see Fig. 8). At the longer end of the visible spectrum is the colour red. Just outside of our vision, past red, are infra-red rays. At the other end, past violet, and also out of the range of average human vision, are the shorter, ultra-violet rays.

Electro-magnetic waves are known to measure several thousand feet from peak to peak at the long end down to the very tiny cosmic rays at the other end.

Modern science and medicine use the waves of almost all parts of the chart from microwaves to x-rays, radio and television broadcasting, telephone and other communications.

X-rays allow us to look into the physical body without the use of surgery and have been used to treat some skin cancers, as radium rays have been used to cure some cancers. Currently medical science is experimenting with the use of even shorter rays to treat disease.

Ultra-violet light is being used in the treatment of cutaneous T-cell leukaemia. A drug called 8-MOP is ingested by the patient. Later the patient's blood is removed and separated into three parts. The parts containing the drug and the patient's white blood cells are combined and subjected to ultra-violet light which causes the drug to attach itself to the diseased cells. The blood is then returned to the patient's body. This treatment has been effective in relieving the disease and getting the patients (who normally would have died within a three-year period) back into normal productive lives.

Ultra-violet radiation has been used as a bactericidal agent for many years to sterilize materials, liquids, and air. We know ultra-violet light is important in preventing rickets and is responsible for the production of vitamin D. This light is situated next to violet light — a light we can actually see — but medical science has decided that the violet frequencies, and of course the whole visible spectrum, is of no medical importance.

As we can see, there are many accepted medical and scientific uses of the various rays on the chart. It is ludicrous to think that visible light is an exception, but until very recently medical science has chosen to ignore and consider useless the tiny band of waves called the visible spectrum. We have only to glance back at the history of the aura and colour therapy in Chapter 7 to see how the established medical community has had an intense aversion to any consideration of the use of coloured light. Yet any plant or animal scientist will tell you that visible light is absolutely essential to the health and very existence of life on this planet.

The importance of full-spectrum light to health has been largely overlooked in our society. Until the last decade or two most of the people in our culture lived in rural areas and worked outside in the rays of the sun. Nowadays over 90 per cent of the workers in the United States work indoors. Most of the lighting in the workplace is not full-spectrum. The latest biological research, such as that of pioneer light-researcher John Ott, has shown that full-spectrum light is crucial to our health and well-being. It has been demonstrated that we need at least fifteen minutes of sunlight daily, absorbed through hands and face, to maintain health. This short exposure helps in keeping vitamin D levels at an appropriate level for calcium metabolism. This is an important fact when we realize that osteoporosis, due to calcium loss, is a very common and serious disease in the Western world. Without sunlight man would have developed in a totally different form, if at all, with no bones.

The most common forms of artificial lighting in the workplace are fluorescent tube lamps. These lamps provide an inexpensive bright light (mostly in the yellow-green range of the spectrum) that does not use as much electricity as a full-spectrum light does. For the sake of economics, workers' health is placed in jeopardy. In the long run the economic consideration is a false one. A worker whose health is marginal because of daily exposure to less than full-spectrum light will have fewer days in the office. This costs the employer in health benefits and work loss.

In an experiment at Cornell University students were given the choice of whether to study under a full-spectrum lamp or the usual fluorescent tube. After only four hours the students who worked under the fluorescent lighting were much more fatigued than those who had chosen full-spectrum. Perhaps those pennies being saved in the workplace could be better spent on the more 'expensive' lighting.

There is also some evidence that tempers will flare more easily in a limited spectrum situation. We have all experienced the tranquillizing effect sunlight has on us. Perhaps workers would be happier and more productive in a full-spectrum office.

The union of psychologists and engineers at the Duro-Test R&D facility in New Jersey has produced an energy efficient artifical full-spectrum light called a Vita-Light. These lights are finding their way into homes and offices all over the country. They are also routinely placed in newborn nurseries at hospitals to reduce the risk of jaundice in the babies.

Dr Ott has produced a full-spectrum light with shielded ends to protect the consumer further from the radioactive emissions in other full-spectrum lights which he believes can be detrimental to health.

Full-spectrum lights are being used to treat another disorder. Many people suffer from a deep state of depression in the winter. A few people are so seriously affected that they commit suicide. This depression comes on in the winter when there is less intense sunlight and people generally stay indoors in northern climates. It is tied up with the secretion of melatonin in the pineal gland. Researchers such as Dr Alfred Lowery of the Oregon Health Sciences University have used daily treatment with full-spectrum lighting on seasonally-depressed individuals with phenomenal success.

Dr Lowery has also used full-spectrum light to treat phase-advanced and phase-delayed sleep disorders. Full-spectrum light applied in the morning for phase-delayed disorders and in the evening for phase-advanced disorders has been successful in adjusting the sleep schedules of those who have to work during standard (9 a.m. — 5 p.m.) work period.

Recent studies with hamsters suffering from heart disease similar to that found in humans, has shown that exposure to twenty-four hours per day of full-spectrum light has increased their life span phenomenally. If this theory can be extrapolated to humans, an extra fifteen years of active and productive life could be given to those who suffer heart disease.

It is difficult to keep up with all of the full-spectrum research that is beginning to blossom around the world. One thing is certain, no longer will the established medical bureaucracy be able to deny the curative powers of the visible spectrum.

Healing and Sealing

Dr John Zimmerman's experiment with a therapeutic touch healer (Chapter 7) showed that healing energy passed from one person to another can be picked up by extremely sensitive EM wave-detection equipment. This healing energy was measured outside of the body, in this case near the head where it was having a restorative effect on the vibratory elements of the inner layers of the aura (health aura).

Several years ago, a talented healer was asked to participate in an experiment at a large US university medical school. In the experiment, two groups of rats had the skin removed from their backs. The first group was treated daily to healing energies sent out of the hands of the healer. The second group was kept away from the healer and only had human contact for feeding. Over a period of weeks the healer's group showed rapid healing, while the other group healed at a more usual rate. With this success in mind, researchers set out to see if some of the medical interns could replicate the experiment. After several weeks of mock healing by the young students (who probably did not believe it was possible to heal in this manner) it was noted that the group which had had no healing (the slower-healing group in the first experiment) were actually healing faster. The interns had retarded the healing process with their negative attitudes!

Any surgical procedure, physical trauma or disease will display disruption in the aura. Often this disturbance will be seen as an area with no auric light present. These holes in the aura permit infections and other complications to develop in the physical area of the injury. The natural healing processes become impeded for a time and healing is slow.

We have found that if, just after surgery, someone can provide a projection of healing energy from his or her hands to the auric layers over the wound, it greatly enhances the healing process. I call this short and simple process 'healing and sealing' the aura. All one has to do is hold the right hand, palm down, over the wound and move the hand in a circular fashion, as if smoothing out wet clay, at each level of the five lower auric layers (see Fig. 9). I usually use a crystal for this purpose as well as my hands because crystals can help to focus the energy. I also project specific colours for the specific problem I am treating. The most important thing is not the colours or crystal, or even working on the various levels of the aura, but that the intention be one of *love*. Love is what powers the energy from the hands, what triggers life back into the empty auric space. All of us can use this process simply by sending love from our hearts out through our hands.

Whenever I mention this technique at one of my lectures I invariably meet with doctors or nurses afterwards who say that they would love to use the method but are afraid the patient or some other medical personnel would catch them performing this 'hocus-pocus'. I always suggest that if they are confronted by the patient or others they should merely say that they are feeling for heat around the incision. They seem to think that this is a good idea.

My wife Carol had to have a small tumour removed from a sensitive spot near the tear duct of her right eye. For several days before surgery she spent time focusing on generating a healing attitude within herself, visualizing the eye already healed. On the day of the surgery a group of friends met and sent her healing energy from a home several miles away from the hospital. Carol insisted on being as clear as she could during the surgery, so she turned down general anaesthesia, opting for a local instead.

After the surgery was performed Carol was wheeled into post-op. recovery where I was waiting dressed in a sterile surgical outfit. I quickly pulled out my corundum crystal and began healing and sealing. Whenever a nurse or doctor came around I palmed the crystal and smiled innocently at them. These days when I appear in post-op. to heal and seal I am totally accepted, no one even looks twice as I work openly with my crystal (see Fig. 10).

Twenty-four hours after the surgery the doctor examined his work and was surprised to find indications that it was healing very rapidly.

Five days after the surgery, Carol was supposed to go in to see if the stitches needed to come out. By the third day after surgery only two of the five stitches were still in place. One had actually flown out of the eye and hit the mirror as she was looking into it! The surgeon examined her eye on the fifth day and was very impressed with the rate of healing. Not only was she healing fast but the scar tissue was nearly non-existent. Prior to surgery, he was certain that there would be a scar. Carol decided to tell him what we had been doing to effect a better healing. He listened, quietly nodding and politely sent her home. At her next visit two weeks later, he was surprised to see the eye had completely healed with no trace of scarring whatsoever. In fact, he had to look at his files to remind himself which eye he had operated on. Carol once again told him about healing and sealing. This time the surgeon requested copies of my documentation and drawings of the eye before, directly after, and up to that day. I had drawn the auric emanations including notes regarding the techniques and visualizations used. He may not have completely grasped what we did but his mind was stretched a little.

Another case in point was an old friend of mine who was best man at our wedding. He was remodelling his kitchen and nearly cut a couple of left-hand fingers off with an electric saw. He had some surgical repair performed on them and after a few weeks of healing the doctor told him they would probably never regain their full motion. My friend was distressed, he had been a fine guitar player and was now unable to use these fingers to play. Carol and I asked if he would let us try to help him. We sat for five minutes or so projecting energy into the fingers and then released and detached from the energy.

My friend's desire to heal and play the guitar again, combined with a 'jump-start' through us, manifested the healing. He is able to play once again to the amazement of his doctor who has taken full credit. The credit really goes out to my friend and his attitude. No one is healed who doesn't accept the healing and stimulate the natural systems of healing within.

To sum up:

1   Healing is a process stimulated by an exchange of love-powered energy.
2   To heal completely, one must deal with the root cause and treat more than just the physical body.
3   The use of visualizations and affirmations can focus the mind on the positive and change negative beliefs and behaviours.
4   Visible light is an important tool in healing through the aura. We would be wise to analyze our living and working environments and make changes where needed.
5   Intent is more important than technique. Anyone with the right attitude can assist in the healing of others as well as themselves.
6   Healing and sealing the aura ensures a prompt and uncomplicated healing period.
7   We are, each of us, ultimately responsible for our own healing just as we are also the sole creators of our disharmonies.

9

How to See Auras

Children and Auric Sight

As a young boy I spent many an hour under a tree daydreaming. In this relaxed state I enjoyed the play of subtle colours around the people I watched. Like most children I had never heard the word 'aura', if I had, I probably would have thought it was the name of a new brand of candy bar.

My parents were not very religious. Spiritual matters amounted to attending funerals, the Easter service and, of course, dropping me and my brother and sister off at church on Sundays so they could finally have some peaceful time alone. Church was always a stifling, boring and at times frightening experience for me. The image of a bleeding man with nails in his hands and feet was scary. The thought that this poor man had a father who seemed to be always angry and ready to burn or drown everybody on the planet was even worse. We knew that this father was invisible and watched us every moment and knew what we did and thought! One day in the future, after a life full of suffering and trying to be nice, I would die and come face to face with him. Then he would decide whether or not I would be thrown into a flaming lake full of screaming people in Hell.

There was a lot of attention paid to Christ's last days on earth. He was beaten up, whipped, made to wear a sharp ring of thorns that caused blood to run all over his face. He had to drag a heavy cross for miles and then they nailed him to it in a thunderstorm. The adults seemed to be obsessed with this man's murder.

I could never understand people's interest in such an image. I liked the Christ in the Sunday school books who had children crawling all over him. He looked so gentle and friendly, someone you'd like to know. He seemed somehow more complete than most of the other characters in the books. He had light all around him. People in the church and on the street had light around them, Mom and Dad had light around them, even my brother and sister had light around them. But the books I read didn't show light around people, even photographs of people were incomplete.

It didn't really bother me that pictures didn't show the light I saw. Most of the time I was busy and I didn't pay much attention to the lights. No one ever talked to me about them and I never thought to talk to anybody about them. They were just part of my reality, my way of perceiving the world, it was as natural as breathing.

I suppose if I had said anything about the lights I would have been told that I was imagining things. When I had 'imaginary' friends, I was told that I was getting to be too old for them and had to start learning to distinguish what was real from what was 'fantasy'. It happened to all my friends as well. One by one we all made our choices about what was real (guided by what our parents and teachers deemed real), and made our passage out of childhood. I'm glad I never mentioned the lights. It is one last remaining treasure of those times that I will always have. If I had said something I'm sure my life would be a lot different today — the lights would have been put out.

My friend Cliff called me a few months ago. His voice was excited. It seems he was having a talk with his four-year-old son Derek about the mechanism of seeing. Cliff is a doctor and a very talented photographer and he was trying to put his extensive knowledge of sight and light into terms a four-year-old could understand. Cliff took Derek to a darkened room to talk about the way the eye adjusts to different light conditions. Derek listened carefully for a while then he matter-of-factly started telling his father what he was seeing in these low-light conditions. He described seeing a blue light around each of the members of his family. He also delineated a ball of glowing light which he said had a name.

Cliff called me immediately to find out if Derek could possibly be seeing auras. It sounded as if he was so I suggested Cliff sit down with him right away and have him draw out what he had seen. Derek likes to draw and colour so it was not very difficult to encourage him to make a drawing; in fact he made five pictures.

One picture depicts the faces of each family member surrounded by envelopes of what he described as blue light (see Fig. 14). At the base of the largest envelope he has drawn a dark spot with radiant lines shooting out at the other envelopes. This is the invisible 'person' Derek described as a ball of light named Sikenfru. He also represented Sikenfru's name on the picture by an 'e' and an 'o' which he said should be o&e. Another picture was a portrait of Sikenfru with radiant lines and the symbol for his name written in the centre of him (see Fig. 15). Cliff carefully wrote down everything Derek had to say about the blue lights and the ball of light called Sikenfru. Several days later they came to our home to visit and Derek proudly showed me his pictures and explained all about them.

Derek is fortunate to have parents who are open-minded and can understand that he has a view into realities that most of us have long forgotten. As Derek grows up he will adjust to the same realities we all share and he will get along just fine in the world but he will always know that he alone creates his reality, and that

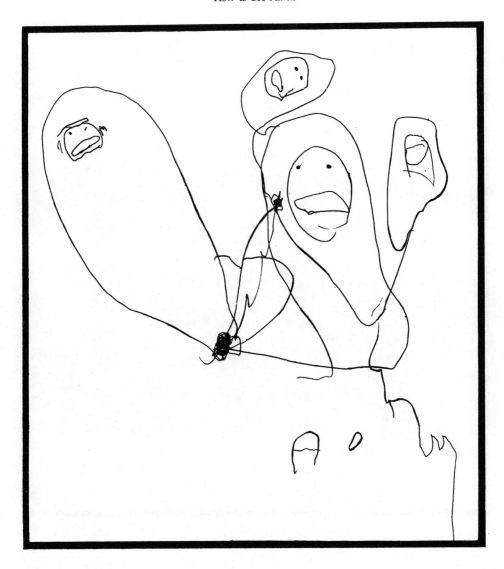

Figure 14 *Four-year-old Derek's family aura drawing. Starting in the upper left-hand corner moving clockwise, Derek's father Cliff, his younger brother Adam, his mother Mary (under Adam), and his newborn sister Allison (with no face, wrapped in a blanket). The figures were all described as being surrounded by blue light. The black scribble (near center) is Sikenfru.*

Figure 15 *Derek's Guide Energy Sikenfru. The lines represent the radiance of the entity. The letters in the centre (supposed to be an 'e' and an 'o') represent the name Sikenfru.*

in this marvellous universe there are endless possibilities and, just perhaps, he will be that much ahead of the game for it.

Good News

Most of us, with the proper training and attitude, can regain the ability to see auras and use our other so-called 'extrasensory perceptions'.

In my workshops I have guided hundreds of people through a visualization geared to train people to see auras.

Before the exercise I ask for a show of hands to find out how many people have already seen what they thought might be an aura. I take note of those who did not raise their hands so I can compare the difference after the process. When the exercise is over I ask the participants to share what they have seen. Inevitably several of those who had never seen an aura report seeing light, and in many cases even colour, around their partner. Those who had seen auras before often report a great deal more than they had seen previously. The ones who had never seen anything before are usually very excited and joyously share every detail. For some of these individuals it is an enormously releasing feeling, as if their vision had been locked away for all of these years just waiting for someone to say it was all right to use it.

How It's Done

In Chapter 1 I described the way in which the eye perceives the aura. Let's recap on the information.

The aura is perceived by our peripheral, not focused, vision. In the receptor field of an eye there are 130 million rod receptors, most of them are located in the periphery of that field. They are low-light receptors, our night vision. Working out from the centre of the field into the rod-receptor zone are some 7 million cone receptors. They are focused-vision receptors and operate best in daylight.

Rod receptors synthesize rhodopsin, also known as visual purple, which is extremely sensitive to subtle light. Low-light conditions are needed to view the aura because it is the rod receptors that image-in the subtle light of auric emanations.

Find a room in your home where you can control the amount of light entering it. Pull down any window blinds. Set two chairs approximately 8 ft (2.5m) apart facing each other. One chair should have its back 2-3 ins (5-7cms) from a wall. The wall should be white or dark with no pictures, shelves or knickknacks. Patterned wallpaper creates difficulties when trying to view the aura and should always be avoided.

I use a non-reflective black cloth to eliminate background distractions and colours.

It measures 6 ft (1.8m) long by 4 ft (1.2m) wide, with a 1½ ins (4cms) diameter dowel rod sewn in at the top and bottom to reduce the bulges and creases when it is hanging. (Bulges in the material will create shadows which can be distracting.) The black cloth is hung (often over a door ledge) by two 's' hooks constructed from a heavy wire. It should drop almost to the floor and extend up several feet above the head of your subject. The back of your subject should be to the cloth, his or her chair should be 2-3 ins (5-7cms) in front of the cloth and centred.

Some people tell me they prefer to use a white background. I find grey to be an excellent background as well. It is important to be consistent with your examinations; because the auric colours are so subtle, any change in background from subject to subject will also change the colours noted slightly. It is best to stay with one background tone and get to know which auric colours are which against it before attempting to make changes.

Several years ago while living in Denver I was asked to attend a psychic fair some sixty-five miles away in Fort Collins where I now live. The organizer of the fair was an energetic wisp of a woman who had taken on the enormous task of raising funds for her metaphysical study group. It was her first fair and she had a lot to learn. One mistake she made, at least as far as I was concerned, was to book a room that had wall to wall windows with no shades, and overhead banks of fluorescent lights that could not be individually turned off. I spent two days at that fair praying, asking God to amplify my auric sight so I could just get through those days. Fluorescent lighting plays havoc with my auric vision as does bright sunlight. At best I would only get the slightest colour detail. I sweated out each reading but all went well thanks to Friends in High places. I was upset with the fair's organizer for her choice of room but she had learned a lot from the experience, as had I. I forgave her and we were married six months later. Carol has organized many fairs since then and always takes lighting into consideration when she selects the locations.

Lighting conditions are crucial to the success of an aura-viewing session, especially for the novice. When you first start out it is best to create optimum viewing conditions. Always be sure that a small amount of light is coming from a source behind you as you sit facing your subject. Natural light is best, either sunlight through a window or candle light. I use a standard light-bulb in a lamp behind me at night so I can see to draw my aura portrait, but most people find candles to be best. When using a candle be sure to eliminate any draughts in the room that might blow the flame around; it can be very distracting to have the shadows moving back and forth across your backdrop. In daylight, adjust the curtains, blinds or shades to your best advantage. It usually takes a few trys to get the light just right for your particular visual needs.

Now drag your husband, wife or friend away from the television and tell him or her you are going to spend some time staring at his or her aura. Of course you will have a better chance of succeeding if your subject is a willing participant. I suggest you find a friend who is interested in trying to see the aura and take turns examining each other's aura.

Turn on some soft, relaxing music. I like to use New Age music such as Steven Halpern's *Spectrum Suite* in which he has designed pieces to fit the vibrations of each of the major colours of the visible spectrum. Make this experience as painless and relaxed as possible.

I always suggest the use of a grounding technique before you attempt any visualization, meditation or aura-viewing session. One such technique is included in the process below.

Both you and your subject should begin by closing your eyes and taking a deep breath to relax. Make sure you are sitting up straight, legs uncrossed, feet flat on the ground. Place your hands on your lap, palms up.

I use the following prayerful technique to begin each examination. It is said silently:

Lord, here I am with another aura to view. Please surround us with a large golden globe of protective Light and fill it with vibrations of positivity, clarity and love. Let nothing disturb or disrupt this work.

Help me now to be grounded. I send beams of light out of the chakras at the bottoms of my feet and from my root chakra and direct them into the centre of the earth. Drawing up earth energy, I anchor myself in this chair. I now ask that my crown chakra be open to receive the blazing gold light of Your positive energies. I now fully accept the responsibility of being a channel for Your positive work.

Help me now to construct an empathic corridor (I envision a rose-covered archway) between myself and this person (the subject) so that I may better understand his/her realities, protecting each of us from each other's negative energies. Allow me now to fully understand what this person is experiencing in his/her life.

Help me to see, draw and interpret quickly those things I need to so I can convey the information this person needs for his/her positive evolvement.

Help me to stay out of the way of this process, to avoid involving my personal feelings or thoughts about what I am perceiving, to provide Your guidance.

Thank you for this opportunity to help this person. For this opportunity, for those to come, and for those of the past, I am grateful.

Amen

Now take a deep breath and as you let it out slowly open your eyes. Do not open them wide; barely open them so you are looking out of a crack through your eyelashes. It helps to tilt the head back and look down your nose. Remember not to focus or try to see the aura. Relax. Be aware to look at the outer edges of your subject.

After a few moments the rhodopsin will bleach off the rod receptors and you will have to close the eyes again to allow it to re-synthesize. When you close your eyes you will probably notice images that have burned into your vision. They will appear as a negative (reverse) image, that is, shapes that were dark with your eyes open will now be light on your inner eyelids. Let these burned-in images melt away as the rhodopsin re-synthesizes, then open your eyes again. Repeat this process as often as you need to.

I recommend keeping a notebook with your observations in it. If you use a subject several times it is interesting to compare notes on changes or similiarities from session to session. Note colours, shapes, feelings, symbols or images that appear to you. Check for rays and guide energies. If you hear something in your head, a word or message, write it down. I have learned to take notes and sketch the aura as I am viewing but if you are a novice you will probably be more focused on the process if you take mental notes and write them down and sketch after the viewing is over.

With practice this technique will strengthen your auric sight. It will become easier each time you do it. Don't be discouraged, it often takes time to develop this technique. Some people will see colours right off and others may just experience a misty grey/blue haze around the subject. In time more will be revealed to those who practise.

Please remember: don't try too hard to see the aura. It is very important to maintain a relaxed attitude. Let it happen, don't force it. When you try too hard you will automatically switch to focused vision. Focused vision will cause a strong burn-in on the receptor field. When the muscles of the eye fatigue the position of the eye will shift slightly and you will see the burned-in image where the aura should be. I call this phenomenon 'the false aura'. The false aura is a flat colour, not translucent like the true aura. It will be the opposite or complement of the colour of the shirt or skin tones of your subject — for instance, a person wearing a red shirt will create a green false aura, a purple shirt will create a yellow false aura, etc.

When viewing the aura be joyous and have fun.

Aids to Develop Auric Sight

Many people have difficulty in trying to visualize colours. They often have to be familiarized and sensitized to the various vibrations of the colours of the spectrum. The following two exercises can be helpful.

Exercise 1

Get two dozen envelopes and number them 1-24. Cut coloured paper or cloth representing the seven major colours of the rainbow into strips small enough to fit into the envelopes. Have someone who is not going to participate in the exercise stuff the swatches into the envelopes, one to an envelope. As this is being done, the person must write down the colour's name and the number of the corresponding envelope. The person (or persons) who will be viewing the sealed envelopes must make a numbered (1-24) list on which to write their impressions about what colours are inside each envelope. Make two columns, one for a first-impression guess (time limit 15 seconds), the other for a long-impression guess (5 minutes maximum).

During the long-impression guess a person might close his or her eyes and hold the envelope between the palms of both hands or hold the envelope against the sixth chakra waiting for an impression. Various individuals will devise different methods of sensing the colours.

When all of the envelopes have been sensed, compare the original list with your answers. Score 5 points for correct first-impression answers, 2 points for correct long-impression answers. If you are doing this exercise alone, compare your scores with previous ones; if you are doing this exercise in a group compare scores and try another round. But remember, this is not a competition. It is an exercise to sensitize you to the vibrations of various colours. Have fun with it and use it to grow.

Exercise 2

Another fun exercise for colour-sensitivity training is to think of a colour and try to project it to another person. This is especially fun in a small group where everyone writes down their guesses. A follow-up to this exercise is to have one person try to project a colour all around him or herself as the others try to see it. Low-light conditions are best for this exercise of course.

Quite often people will tell me that they don't have anybody to use as a subject to practise aura-viewing. I like to tell them that's good news — now they have a great opportunity to go out and make a friend of someone else who is interested in metaphysical matters! But until then, you can practise using your own two hands.

Our hands are important senders and receivers of energy, the concentration of energy is great in and around them. The auric emanations are likewise very strong at the hands, making them easier to see than many other parts of the aura (excluding the area around the head). In the same low-light conditions you would use to view another person, hold your hand out at arms length against your backdrop and view it using the methods described above. After a while get closer to the hand (10ins from your face) and look closely between the fingers and at the fingertips. You should see energy pouring out from the tips. Note also a thin band

($\frac{1}{16}$-$\frac{1}{8}$ in (1-3mm) wide) of light blue/grey immediately next to the skin; this is the physical auric body. There is much to be seen around the hands. They are a good place to start for any beginner.

There is a classic exercise first introduced by Oscar Bagnall which has been used by teachers of the aura ever since. It is very simple. Place your hands palms down on the backdrop with the fingertips touching. Then, slowly pulling the hands apart, note the lines of energy still connecting the fingertips. The sceptic will say that the lines are an optical illusion. To dispel that notion, move one hand higher and the other hand lower (see Figs. 11a and 11b) and look again at the connections at the fingertips.

It is fun to create aura-viewing exercises of your own. The more you can create positivity and happiness when you work with the aura, the more likely you are to see and understand about it.

Aura Portraits

I have mentioned my aura portraits several times in this book. Aura portraits are my way of collecting data and supplying it to the subject in a form that is immediately understandable.

The pictures in my Sunday school books when I was a child seemed incomplete to me because I knew people were more than that. We are Beings of Light living temporarily in a fleshly body.

An aura portrait (see Fig. 12) shows the complete person, as we really are.

I have included an actual aura portrait here (the face is changed to protect the identity of the subject) for the reader to use to practise analysis. By now you will have gleaned enough information to begin. As you practise aura-viewing and analysis you may want to create aura portraits of your subjects. All it takes is the ability to draw (which I believe can be taught to almost everybody — it's a technical skill like any other) and a willingness to work at seeing auric emanations. Add to that a desire to be in touch with the natural intuitive side of yourself and it can be done.

In all of my travels on the lecture circuit I have yet to find someone who could do my aura portrait. Perhaps one day I will meet one of you who has practised and developed this talent and I will finally get an aura portrait of my own.

10

Creating the New Age

When we released the energy from the atom, everything changed. . .except our way of thinking. Because of that we drift toward unparalleled disaster. We shall require a substantially new manner of thinking if mankind is to survive.

Albert Einstein

What did Einstein mean by 'a new manner of thinking'? I believe he was talking about Universal Love. Universal Love is a soul-felt understanding that we and all that we perceive on this planet and beyond to the limits of our imagination are One. We are our neighbours, we are the trees and rocks and water. We are the air and all that has ever been thought or created. Universal Love means we are linked at every level of our being. No thought or action occurs that doesn't affect every other element in the universe. When we hurt others, we are hurting ourselves. When a child in Ethiopia is dying of starvation, we are dying. When we create joy and positivity, we all reap the benefits.

It is illusion to believe we are separate from all others, that we are more intelligent or more beautiful than the lowest form of life. These divisions are self-made; they are destructive beliefs, destructive to our survival and to the survival of all things.

There is a New Age on the horizon, an age when our collective consciousness will finally join together to understand the connection we have to the cosmos. The New Age is inevitable, it conforms to natural laws, it is evolution.

We stand poised at a crossroads in our evolution. It is a time of careful choices; do we choose to live. . .or to die? When we choose to recognize the unity of all things then our choice is brotherhood and a positivity that generates peace, both personal and world-wide. If we continue to generate a consciousness of separateness we will continue to be at odds with each other, and will eventually destroy ourselves.

The New Age will be created one consciousness at a time. Isn't it time to choose a new way of thinking that allows positivity and harmony to flourish? We can eliminate dis-ease and disharmony, strife and greed, but we must choose now or all that we are and all we have created will cease to be, as we know it, and consciousness will find new channels through which to express itself and evolve.

To those hardened individuals who say that the notion of a New Age is too idealistic, I say 'Why do you choose to limit your potential?' We are limitless beings and we can create whatever we put our minds to. Just look at what we've created so far; some of it is incredibly beautiful; some of it reflects our negativity and flawed thinking, but we did it all so well! We can begin now to make positive choices and use that same incredible power to turn things around. We must start with the belief that it is possible; that's the first step. Without that belief we haven't got a chance. Those who can't accept the possibility have dead-ended their potential and condemn themselves to the old cycles of fear, hatred and death of spirit.

Singer-composer, John Lennon said it best in his song *Imagine*: the chorus says: 'You may say I'm a dreamer, but I'm not the only one. Perhaps one day you'll join us and the world will live as one.'

Forgiveness

The study of the aura shows us that we are more than we may have previously thought we were. We can see how we can be interconnected by our thoughts, our auric bodies and chakras. We have seen we can heal ourselves and others by the projection of our energies through these channels. By understanding the mechanics of how we create our reality and how we can improve on it, we realize that we can create a better world as well.

To move into the future in the most positive way we must first learn how to deal with the past and eliminate the unhealthy aspects of it so that we can finally be free to go on. One thing paramount to that process is learning to forgive and release past events that hold us in our old patterns. By hanging on to negative feelings such as resentment we are only feeding our anger, and anger feeds on us. When we eliminate these negative feelings we clean out harmful thought-forms from the aura and we generate mental, emotional, spiritual and physical health and well-being.

Forgiveness is fundamental to the teachings of Jesus. It is the door by which we can enter the kingdoms of peace and harmony, yet there are very few today who profess to be Christians who actually practise the kind of forgiveness Jesus talked about nearly 2000 years ago. Wars generated in the name of Christianity litter our history books because of the inability to forgive and go on.

Acceptance of life's events without judgement is fundamental to Buddhist belief which avoids the build-up of the anger and resentment that leads to a need for forgiveness.

We've had the answers for years but they were cloaked in ceremony and philosophy. The answers rattled around in our heads on the intellectual level but rarely reached our hearts where the real healing is needed.

There is a simple yet effective technique that can be employed to release us from the past so we can continue to evolve unimpeded by negativity. It is a visualization I call the 'Let Go and Grow' process.

This process will take a little preparation. You will need to find a quiet place where you won't be disturbed. If you do it right you will experience great emotional release. Begin by sitting in a comfortable chair. Use a grounding technique and take a few deep breaths to relax. Have a piece of paper and a pencil handy. We will be exploring events that occurred a long time ago in your childhood; go as early into your childhood as you can to examine the roots of the behaviour problems that you suffer from today. Most often this is where our self-image was constructed and the negative tapes were created.

For example, let's say you often feel worthless and unwanted. Write down on your paper, 'I often feel worthless and unwanted'. Now ask yourself how this interferes with living up to your highest potential and write the answers down. Remember, no one else is ever going to see your answers if you choose not to share them, so be as blunt and to the point as you can. If you participate 100 per cent in this process you will benefit 100 per cent.

Begin to reflect on those images from the past that bring up painful feelings of being worthless and unwanted. Focus on the exact instances and try to be detached enough to see the details. Where were you? How old were you? Who was there with you? What feelings did you have then? What feelings do you have now? Quickly jot down the answers to these questions and move on to another time which might be related in some way to your present-day feelings of being unwanted and worthless and ask the questions again.

Some of us will have no trouble recalling the specifics of the root of the problem, others will have locked many of the painful memories away and will have to try a few times to detail the events. The memories are not lost; they are there in the subconscious mind and can be recalled enough to work with. The subconscious mind uses the memory and subsequent like-memories to form and reinforce your negative belief about yourself all day long so you can bet it's in there. If an image is foggy, or you're just not sure how it goes, don't worry about it, work with what you've got. You'll be surprised how much will come back if you just continue.

The information gathered in the preparation part of this process will be a road map for the next part. You may want to rest between the first part and second part, and you can of course do so, but I suggest striking while the iron is hot. Now that you have dredged up the past it's most beneficial to go with what you are feeling.

If you take a rest, refresh your memory about what you are working on by rereading your notes. Relax and close your eyes. Take several deep breaths, breathe out tension, and ground yourself.

In your mind's eye envision a theatre marquee: your name is on it in the starring role. Today's special matinée is an episode from your childhood. As you buy your ticket and enter you pass a sign: 'It is the policy of this theatre to give our audiences only plays that have happy endings'.

You pass through a velvet curtain and walk to the front of the empty theatre to the best seat in the house. The lights dim and the curtains slide apart. A solitary spotlight fades up on a young child on the stage. It is you at the age you were in the first event you mapped in the first part of this process. Let's call you Emily for the sake of this example. While you were delving into the past you remembered that your father used to get extremely angry with you for what you perceived as 'no reason at all'. Bring your father on stage. He enters your spotlight in a rage.

FATHER   Emily! How many times have I told you to leave my books alone? You're going to ruin them. Your hands are filthy and now look at this book. I've had it! (*Father pulls the book out of Emily's hand and slaps her across the face. She begins to cry.*) 'I'm sick and tired of having to watch you all the time, you can't be trusted. Why aren't you helping your mother with the dishes, you **worthless** brat? It's no wonder you don't have any friends, **who'd want a friend like you?** Always destroying other people's property. . .

EMILY   But Daddy, I was only looking at. . .

FATHER   (*interrupting*) Shut up and get out of here. (*He chases after her and she falls trying to get away. He raises his hand to hit her again when. . .*)

From the audience, experiencing the pain, you see yourself standing up, and at the top of your lungs you yell, 'Stop'! The characters freeze where they are.

Sometimes it's good to actually yell out loud during this part of the exercise as long as you can maintain the visualization and continue.

See yourself as you look today, running up onto the stage. Go over to little Emily and hold her, comforting her. Cry along with her, feel her emotion, feel your emotion. You may want to actually hug yourself as you experience this scene. Go ahead and get into the emotion of it, you're alone, there is no one there to judge you. Experience these emotions completely, it will help you to release the pain.

Little Emily is too young to understand that her father is frustrated and worried about money and is taking it out on her. Perhaps he feels insecure because he doesn't think he is able to take care of his family properly. He is feeling shame for his inadequacies. He is seeing himself as worthless as he enters the room and sees Emily getting fingerprints on a valuable book and he projects what he's feeling about himself onto her.

You, the adult Emily, can understand these things; you've probably had similar problems yourself. But little Emily had no idea what was going on. All she knew is that she wanted to look at the book that her father cherished. She never thought to wash her hands, she's only five years old and sometimes forgets some of the rules — there are so many. Her father entered and was very angry. He told her that she was 'worthless' and asked 'who would ever want you for a friend'? 'He must be right,' thinks little Emily, sobbing, 'after all he's my Daddy and he knows everything.' If this scene is repeated a few times little Emily will begin to form a negative self-image.

Let's return to the visualization. You are comforting little Emily. You dry her tears, stand up and walk over to your father. He is still frozen but he can see and hear you. You say, 'Father, I understand some of your frustrations. I am an adult now too and I have had some of the same problems but little Emily doesn't understand. All she knows is that the person who is in charge of guiding her life has just told her she is worthless and could never have a friend and she believes it! I believed it for many years as I grew up and it has caused me to dislike myself, and to be friendless. But I am taking charge of my life now and to do that I am about to change this event from my past.'

The next part of this process is very important, it is the crux of the mechanism, the part that makes it work. There are three things that must be said to the father (in this example), and little Emily (your child self). They are:

1 I, (use your first name here), completely forgive you for. . .
2 I love you.
3 I completely release you from. . .

These simple statements are powerful, they change the past as you say them. Always remember you are forgiving yourself when you forgive the child. Little Emily represents the child that lives within adult Emily.

Emily now walks up to father and puts her arms around him (no matter what kind of emotion you are currently feeling toward the person you are forgiving, this action in the visualization is very important). She hugs him, holding him for a while and sending love to him. Then she pulls back, still holding him so that she can look him in the eyes. With all of the heartfelt emotion she can muster she says, 'Father, I now forgive you for all of the things you have said and done to me over the years that have hurt me. . .And I love you. . . (at this point, look into the eyes as you speak. See the shocked expression, see the tears well up. Now make the person respond as you have always wished he or she would. This is your play, you can make it any way you want to.) . . . and I completely release you from any guilt or shame you may have acquired from all this.' She now gives him a last hug and walks over to little Emily.

She now repeats the same three sentences to little Emily. 'Emily, I completely forgive you for hating Father all these years. . .I love you. . .and I release you from the guilt and pain you have suffered from all these years.' Hold her in your arms and cry. Feel the release, the peace of mind settling in. Now envision the three of you walking off the stage arm in arm in love and harmony finally. The curtain closes. Relax and sleep for a while.

Use this process to 'Let Go and Grow' as often as you need to. Go after all of your life's events that caused pain and make them right. This powerful visualization works. It is one of the few tools that I have come across that permanently removes old thought-forms from the astral auric body.

Affirmations

Most of us have heard of or used affirmations in some form or other in our lives. They are an excellent tool to reinforce new belief systems. I suggest you use them in conjunction with the above process. An affirmation will help over-ride old tapes, eventually replacing negative beliefs or behaviours with positive ones.

Many of you have tried affirmation exercises in the past with little or no success. People have told me many of the methods they have used that have failed. Often their affirmations were too long and/or they simply gave up before the effects could be noticed. Others have reported negative effects from affirmations. We must be careful to word our affirmations in a positive-generating way. The most common trait of a non-effective affirmation was that it was used for too short a period of time. Some people said they were told it would work in seven days, others said twenty-one days or thirty days. The behaviours, beliefs and attitudes that we are trying to change took many years to grow within us, and it takes a massive effort to over-ride them.

My plan of affirming works. I have used it very successfully in my own life. It is much the same as many other methods with two exceptions; one, I have extended the length of time the affirmation is used; two, I have shortened the length of the wording of the affirmation.

Because of the time the old tapes have had to become engrained in our subconscious mind I find it takes a long time to over-ride them. I have shortened the length of the affirmation because I believe a person will be more likely to stick with it if it is shorter. A long affirmation will very likely be discarded after a week or two because it becomes cumbersome. The ego looks for any reason it can find not to change the status quo and a long affirmation is a good excuse to stop the process.

The affirmation process is simple in design. The first step is to create a concise, positive statement that says what you would like to be or have. It is important to create the statement so it says what you want to have happen as if it has already happened. For example, let's take the case of Emily above. Emily feels worthless and unworthy of anyone's love or friendship. A good affirmation for Emily would be, 'I am worthwhile and worthy of friendships'. The 'I am' suggests to the subconscious it is already true. To say 'I will be worthwhile and worthy of friendships' puts it in the ever-moving, elusive future — it will never be attained in the present. Notice that Emily's affirmation is not flowery like some affirmations you may have tried. It is concise and to the point. Be aware of your wording and chop out all of the extra words'. I am a child of God with the right to feel worthwhile and express His abundant love through loving and worthwhile friendships' is a nice affirmation, but how many times per day can you repeat it before it becomes a burden?

The next step is to put your affirmation to work. Repeat the statement, with feeling, two hundred times per day. It seems like an impossible task, but it is not. If you drive to work in the morning you can easily do fifty affirmations in the few minutes it takes to get there. Fifty more at lunch and you are halfway there. If you do fifty more before dinner and another fifty when you lie down to sleep you've done it. If you are like me you'll probably get through the day and realize at bedtime you haven't done one all day. Don't fret; in the evening just before sleep is one of the most receptive times for your subconscious mind to accept the new tape. I found I could run through all 200 of my affirmations in around twenty minutes. At the end of the twenty minutes I was very relaxed and could fall asleep easily (good news for insomniacs). It is important not to get all hung up on counting each affirmation — it makes it frustrating and interferes with the full strength of the process. To remedy this I created a small string of fifty beads. Then all I had to do was move a bead as I said the affirmation. When I had been around the circle four times I was finished.

When you first start with a new affirmation it is good to say it out loud for the first fifty or so. Put as much feeling as you can into what you are saying. As time goes on you will be able to say them in your head very quickly. If you should happen to miss a day, or perhaps only get through 50 or 100, don't worry about it. Forget it and do the next day's affirmation in full. We tend to punish ourselves internally if we don't make our target and that is not necessary. After all, what we are trying to do here is heal our problems not add to them.

The third step is for the affirmations to continue for a full three months. Remember we are dealing with long-standing behaviour and it takes time to clear it out. How long is three months of commitment compared to all the years of suffering under the old message? It is a very small amount of time compared with the enormous benefits.

Here is a scenario of the typical events of the affirmation process.

The first week or two Emily works diligently at it, never missing an affirmation. Then she starts to hear this little voice in her head saying, 'This is stupid, it's not working'. At that point she wants to give up or she starts slipping on getting them done, until one day she almost sabotages the whole thing. Determined, she decides to hang in there. The fact that she felt like stopping shows that the ego was being affected. It doesn't want to change so it gets panicky and tries to stop her. If Emily can remember to be strong and continue with her commitment to change she can get through this rough period. After a month she would start to see results from the affirmations; she would begin to see that she was appreciated and worthwhile. She may even have attracted new friends by then with her new positive attitude. Of course at the point the ego will say, 'Ok, that's good enough, it worked so we can stop now, we don't have to go through the next two months'. That is a danger signal. If Emily were to stop at that point she may not have had enough time to have created a lasting image in the subconscious, the old tapes could still rear their ugly heads and back she would go. Again, if she can hang in there (she's come too far to go back now, look what she's already accomplished) she will get to a point where the weeks will move along rapidly. Emily's affirmation will become a regular part of her routine like brushing her teeth. Her co-workers will begin to notice positive changes in her, they will like to spend more time with her. Emily will begin to realize she really *is* a worthwhile person and that she is in fact popular with a great many people. Emily will reach the end of her third month without even noticing that the period is over. The true test of when it is time to stop the affirmation is when you don't want to stop because it has become a 'friend', an important part of your day.

After the third month you will be excited to see what else you want to correct. Create a new affirmation and continue. If you ever feel the need to use an old affirmation once in a while, go ahead and do so.

To recap the process: create a concise positive statement that sets out the information you want to replace the old tape with as if it were true now. Say the affirmation 200 times per day for three months. Be committed, and watch out for the slick sabotage techniques of the ego. This technique works. In combination with the 'Let Go and Grow' process you will be well on your way to breaking the stronghold of the past, you will be free to create a new consciousness for the New Age.

The Protective Aura

In Chapter 6 I promised to tell you about the protective aura. I said then that it would possibly be the most important piece of information in this book. To get the most out of this life it is important to participate with a positive attitude. Positivity draws positive events and positive people to you. With a positive outlook the possibilities for attaining your highest potential can be realized. Negative thoughts, beliefs and resulting actions limit potential and draw painful situations into your life. We create our own reality with every moment; the choices we make, be they positive or negative, create a corresponding positive or negative next moment. Once we realize that we always have the choice between those two realities in any given moment a great responsibility confronts us. If we are logical people who care whether we have a quality life filled with possibilities then the choice is simple; we must choose positivity.

I can still remember the moment that I realized we have only two choices in all situations. I was twenty years old and struggling with a series of setbacks in my life. I was walking across a high pile of lumber that had been stored behind my father's barn. The realization hit me like a bolt of lightning, I nearly fell off the lumber pile. It was so simple: since I was creating my own reality by my decision to accept the positive or the negative, it was ludicrous and harmful to accept less than the positive in my life. But knowledge is one thing, putting that knowledge to work is quite another.

It was fifteen years later before I was finally able to begin to practise what I was preaching. I had cashed in twelve years of life and struggle in Tucson, Arizona and moved to Denver, Colorado, a thousand miles from friends and family. When I arrived I had one friend, a young woman who was a beautiful and talented artist. For one happy month she showed me the city and shared her home. It was autumn and the leaves were blazingly beautiful, the air was turning crisp and we were happy friends.

Our days were filled with her costume design projects and we sat for hours talking and sewing sequins. I lent her money to fund a Hallowe'en showing of her costumes and she talked me into dancing in the show as a fire-ball throwing wizard.

But the stress seemed to be changing her personality. She began to act irrationally, talking about plots against her, so after the costume show I moved out and found an apartment several blocks away. I found a job and decided to buy a car she had for sale so I could get to work.

Two weeks passed and my friend's behaviour became more and more bizarre. I knew then that she was mentally ill. Her aura was distorted and caused fear within me whenever I was near her. The relationship had become intolerable.

Life went on in a usual way, off to work, come home, eat and sleep until one night, when my friend's father came over to tell me that he would not tolerate me threatening his daughter and if it continued he would settle with me personally. I was shocked. I hadn't even seen her yet I was supposed to have threatened her life. I tried to explain but he wouldn't listen and stormed off into the night.

One night my friend came over. She was crying and begged me to allow her to stay the night. I reluctantly agreed, I couldn't turn away a friend in such need. She seemed to be calm for a while and then she became extremely paranoid claiming I was a CIA agent who had been bought out by the Mafia and was trying to kill her.

I kept one eye open all night waiting for her to do something crazy. But the evening passed and with the morning she left.

The next day at work I found out the company was going out of business and I needn't return. That began a long period of unemployment. I finally spent all of my savings, then the car I had bought from my friend ceased to operate. I took the car back to her father and he kept it to fix. I never saw it again.

I had not shipped my furniture or other belongings up from Tucson so my small apartment was barren. I was sleeping in a sleeping bag on the floor. The rent was overdue, I was unemployed, hungry and feeling things couldn't possibly get worse, but they did.

One evening the bell rang. It was my friend. She looked mentally very healthy (she was masking her true feelings). I let her in and discovered she had brought me two hot roast-beef sandwiches smothered in gravy. I was famished for food other than the potatoes I had been subsisting on so I eagerly devoured the first sandwich. I was in the middle of the second when I realized I had been poisoned.

I spent the better part of the next two days in a cold sweat, too weak to move, with heart racing. I thought I was going to die. Finally it passed and for several days I sat alone in my apartment, crying and depressed. I was as low as I could go, I didn't know how I was going to survive.

Then I remembered a visualization technique called the protective aura. It was touted in the literature as a powerful protection device that had been demonstrated by Indian fakirs to stop bullets shot from elephant guns. I decided to put it to use. How could I lose? I was so miserable at this point, wallowing in depression and self-pity, that I would have tried anything.

It worked immediately. I felt much more positive and hopeful. After a week of using it my life was already turning around. Shortly thereafter I heard about Carol's psychic fair in Fort Collins and the rest is history, positive history.

If you begin to use this technique tomorrow and practise it faithfully for seven days I guarantee that it can change your life too. The protective aura technique helps you to create positivity in your life and, as I have said, positivity draws the positive to you.

One of the nice things about this visualization is that it can be done anywhere — at home, in a crowd, at the office, on the bus, anywhere. You do not necessarily have to close your eyes to do it, although it may be helpful when you first begin to try it. After you've mastered the basic idea, you can use it instantly at will.

The protective aura is great to use when someone wants to argue with you or

in some other way try to disrupt your peace. It has been especially importan
me to train myself to be 'in the moment'. I have always had a tendency to drift
off into the tense and sometimes frightening future in my mind, or to refight old
battles in the cumbersome past. The use of the protective aura demands your
presence in the everlasting present where it is safe and peaceful.

This is how it's done. Imagine all of your current negative thoughts and fears
and temporarily step away from them. You can leave them for a moment, you
don't have to have every waking moment filled with this stress. Decide for at least
one minute of your day you can be free of it.

This will be your momentary escape. Imagine you have just put all of the mental
trash you have been carrying around into a paper bag. Now toss it over into the
corner of the room and let it go from your mind. The next few moments are a
gift to yourself. Inhale a large amount of air and scream (at the top of your lungs
or silently if you are in the office) TIME OUT! and mean it. With that, take a very
deep breath and hold it for a count of five, then slowly release it, letting go of
any remaining tension and relax. On your next inhalation imagine your body is
covered in a beautiful metallic gold foil. As you exhale this time, see this gold foil
blowing up like a balloon. Envision it surrounding the outer edges of your aura.
Gold is the ultimate protective colour in the physical realm; its reflectiveness and
purity keep all negative externals from entering into your aura. The only place
negativity can now enter is from you within the golden envelope. Fill the interior
of this safe golden cocoon with the beautiful effervescent, rainbow light of positivity.
Inhale the cooling, soothing positivity and relax. This is your time for yourself.
In here you are safe now, protected from external negativity. Feel the relief.

There is a catch however. A negative thought from you will bring this safe cocoon
crashing down and it must be rebuilt. You can rebuild it easily by simply breathing
out a new one and filling it with positivity once again. As you can see, when you
first start using this technique you will be spending a great deal of time making
new protective auras.

I struggled with my negativity for an hour or two (I had a lot to work with at
the time) but then I began to notice I was extending my positive time-period to
several minutes. It was then I had the soul-felt realization that I could step out
of my problems and live in the moment. I knew if I could create positivity for
a few minutes I could do it for an hour or even more. I stuck with it for a full
week, each day extending the periods of time away from negativity. Since I was
away from my problems my mind was able to feel hopeful and solutions to them
began to enter my mind. It was like cleaning a blocked-up drainpipe — suddenly
the old backed-up water rushed out and it was clear. By the seventh day I was
able to maintain my positivity for an hour or two. I would put on my protective
aura and go outside for walks. I saw everything from a new perspective. Trees and

buildings took on a new light, they seemed alive and I, too, finally felt alive. Soon after I began this programme, I found that positive things began to roll my way. I have used this technique ever since.

One use of this protection is in the workplace. Often we are under a lot of pressure to perform and sometimes we have to deal with an angry associate or customer. Simply construct the protective aura around you. Since you are now in a peaceful, positive state of mind you cannot enter into the angry person's game. You can respond from the cocoon but all of your responses will be positive. You will remain untouched. The angry person will eventually run out of steam because it takes two to have an argument. He or she will see you smiling back warmly and the fire will go out (see Fig. 13).

I had to walk through a dark forest at night without a light sometime back. I was alone and I found my hearing and imagination had teamed up to have a little fun with me. After a while my fears had reached a point of no return. The Rocky Mountains can be deadly if you are not prepared and I wasn't. I wanted to run but that would have been dangerous. Instead I created my protective aura and immediately created peace for myself. I was no longer sending out fear all around me which could have attracted danger, instead I was walking in harmony, at one with the night and forest.

The protective aura is a visualization that creates positive thinking in an individual. Positive thinking is the key to the raising of consciousness and the way to create the New Age within your heart.

Psychics in the New Age

I have long had a dislike for the word 'psychic'. It creates a rather negative image in the minds of those who know nothing about what it is and it also puts some people who have developed the talent on pedestals, setting them apart from the rest of us. Because of those reasons the term 'psychic' is long overdue for a change. It does not serve the New Age movement, it only alienates and separates people.

A psychic, says the dictionary, is a person who is especially susceptible to psychic influences. While that may be true it removes a certain group from the mainstream of humanity. I don't believe psychism is unique to only some individuals. We all have and use these abilities to varying degrees in our lives. Some of us focus on and develop these talents and therefore become counsellors for others. Any good psychic will tell you that ultimately you are your own best psychic counsellor if you will only take the time to develop your ability.

As consciousness continues to gather as a group or planetary consciousness, as Teilhard de Chardin, this century's greatest theologian contends, we will join ourselves to each other in the final realization that we are one. This will mark the end of the childhood of man and we will begin a New Age.

The New Age will be a time when all people will be so interconnected 'psychically' that when a need arises in a brother or sister, it will be recognized and remedied with the help of all others. Psychics will be put out of business, as what was deemed unique to only a few becomes common to all.

I for one will be happy when that time comes and I can hang up my coloured pencils and crystal, put my feet up and fully live out the rest of this life knowing that in my own little way I did my best and contributed to the quickening of the evolvement of world consciousness.

One day all students must learn that as the days of the attainment of knowledge end, the moment of BEING begins and our lives are finally complete.

Bibliography

Asimov, Isaac *Understanding Physics: Light, Magnetism and Electricity* Signet, New York, NY, 1969.

Babbitt, Edwin D. *The Principles of Light and Color* published by the author, East Orange, NJ, 1896.

Bagnall, Oscar *The Origin and Properties of the Human Aura* E.P. Dutton & Co., New York, NY, 1937.

Birren, Faber *Color Psychology and Color Therapy* The Citadel Press, Secaucus, NJ, 1950.

Birren, Faber *The Story of Color* Crimson Press, Westport, CT, 1941.

Brain/Mind Bulletin 'New technologies detect effects of healing hands' September 30, 1985.

Burr, H.S. and Northrop, F.S.C. 'The electrodynamic theory of life' *Quarterly Review of Biology,* 10:322, 1935.

Burr, H.S. *Blueprint For Immortality: The Electric Patterns of Life* Neville Spearman, 1972.

Buscaglia, Leo F. *Love* Slack Incorporated, Thorofare, NJ; dist. Morrow, New York, NY, 1986.

Carr, Archie and the Editors of *Life Magazine Life Nature Library: The Reptiles* Time Life Books, New York, NY.

Cayce, Edgar with Sugrue, Thomas *Auras* The Association for Research and Enlightenment, Virginia Beach, Virginia, 1945.

de Chardin, Pierre Teilhard *The Phenomenon of Man* Harper & Row, New York, NY.

Ghadiali, Dinshah P. *Spectro-Chrome Metry Encyclopedia* Spectro-Chrome Institute, Malaga, NJ, 1939.

Health Research *The Aura and What it Means to You* Health Research, Mokelumne Hill, CA.

Innovation: Lighting The Way television programme PBS, WNET/13, New York, NY, 1985.

Jacobi, Jolande (editor) and Guterman, Norman (translator) *Paracelsus: Selected Writings* Pantheon Books, New York, NY, 1951.

Jampolsky, Gerald G. *Love is Letting Go of Fear* Celestial Arts, Millbrae, CA, 1979.

Joy, W. Brugh *Joy's Way* St Martin's Press, J.P. Tarcher Inc., Los Angeles, CA, 1979.

Kilner, Walter J. *The Human Atmosphere* Rebman Co., New York, NY, 1911.

Leadbeater, C.W. *Man Visible and Invisible* Theosophical Publishing Society, London, 1905.

Leadbeater, C.W. and Besant, Annie *Thought Forms* Theosophical Publishing Society, London.

MacIver, Virginia and LaForest, Sandra *Vibrations* Samuel Weiser Inc., York Beach, ME, 1979.

Mille, Julie Ann 'Eye to (Third) Eye' *Science News*, Vol. 128, November 9, 1985.

Ostrander, Sheila and Schroeder, Lynn *Handbook of Psychic Discoveries* Berkley Medallion Books, New York, NY, 1974.

Ott, John N. *Health and Light: The Effects of Natural and Artificial Light on Man and Other Living Things* Devin-Adair Co., Old Greenwich, CT, 1973.

Pancoast, S. *Blue and Red Light* J.M. Stoddart & Co., Philadelphia, PA, 1877.

Raschke, Carl 'Biomagnetism promises sharper brain images' *Colorado Business*, May, 1985.

Regush, Nicholas *The Human Aura* Berkley Books, New York, NY, 1977.

Robinson, Lytle *Edgar Cayce's Story of the Origin and Destiny of Man* Coward, McCann and Geoghegan, New York, NY, 1972.

Science News 'Biology — pineal gland speaks to brains' Vol. 129, 1986.

Young, J.Z. *The Life of Vertebrates* Clarendon Press, Oxford, Oxford University Press, 1981.

Zimmerman, John 'The brain — MEG gets inside your head' *Psychology Today*, April, 1982.

Index